# X-Teams

# X-Teams

*How to Build Teams That Lead,*

*Innovate, and Succeed*

Deborah Ancona and
Henrik Bresman

Harvard Business School Press

*Boston, Massachusetts*

Library of Congress Cataloging-in-Publication Data

Ancona, Deborah G. (Deborah Gladstein)
  X-teams : how to build teams that lead, innovate, and succeed /
Deborah Ancona and Henrik Bresman.
    p. cm.
  ISBN-13: 978-1-59139-692-5 (hardcover : alk. paper)
  ISBN-10: 1-59139-692-1
  1. Teams in the workplace—Management.  I. Bresman, Henrik.
II. Title.
  HD66.A518 2007
  658.4'022-dc22

                                        2007010709

*To our own X-team cores:*

*Henry, Marisa, Anna, Laura, Bertie, and Fama*

*and*

*Annie, Karin and Bertil, Katarina and Martin*

# CONTENTS

ACKNOWLEDGMENTS

F IRST AND FOREMOST we would like to thank our X-teams—
those featured in the book and those that we've studied and
worked with over the years. You have been the catalyst for our theory building, and you have brought the theory to life in your X-team projects. You
have inspired us with your work and spirit, your enthusiasm, and your
great ideas and innovations. Thank you for taking us along on the ride.

We would also like to thank the companies that have let us come in
to observe, work, and experiment. To BP, CVRD, Merrill Lynch, Microsoft,
and NewsCorp, and others that have shown us how context affects teams,
thanks for letting us in.

We owe a great intellectual debt to David Caldwell, who helped to
build the theoretical foundations of this book. Thanks also to David for
being a great friend and coauthor, and for making it all fun.

We want to thank our academic mentors and colleagues who have
helped us to get where we are today. From Deborah, thanks to David
Nadler who provided access to the nursing teams and sales teams, and
who provided guidance and then let me learn on my own. David also
showed me the benefits of linking practice and theory. Thanks to Richard
Hackman for helping us to push the theoretical envelope and for the wisdom. Thanks to Michael Tushman for mentoring and friendship over the
long term and John Anderson for transitioning to publication mode. Thanks
to Peter Kolesar for saying that it couldn't be done and then motivating
me to do it. Thanks to the faculty and my fellow doctoral students at

Columbia for all their help and support. Thanks to Sue Ashford and Jim Walsh for helping through those early academic years and to the Tuck School for all its support of the research. At MIT, thanks to Don Lessard for creating the architecture for X-teams and to Andrew Lo for opening doors and believing. Thanks to Lotte Bailyn for advice and being there when needed.

For Henrik, Deborah is not only coauthor and a friend, but long before the writing of this book, she was also the best academic mentor any doctoral student could have. Many grateful thanks goes to Amy Edmondson, who during those early days argued implausibly that "it can be done" and who has continued to be an incomparable source of inspiration, support, and friendship. Thanks to Örjan Sölvell and the late Gunnar Hedlund for giving the encouragement to take a closer look at an academic career and to Julian Birkinshaw for providing the inspiration to seriously pursue it. Thanks to Eleanor Westney for generously opening the doors to MIT and to all the extraordinary mentors found inside those doors: Tom Allen, Lotte Bailyn, Paul Carlile, John Carroll, Eric Rebentisch, George Roth, JoAnne Yates, and many more. Thanks to Matthew Bidwell, Forrest Briscoe, Sarah Kaplan, Andrew von Nordenflycht, Isabel Fernandez-Mateo, and Sean Safford, who helped manage that dreaded post-examination slump and who have continued to provide priceless support, friendship, and canny advice ever since. Thanks to all fellow doctoral students at MIT and to my nonpareil colleagues at INSEAD. Outside the Ivory Tower, Syd Peterson has helped make the mysteries of drug development much less mysterious. Bob Myers has been an invaluable steward on forays into the world of licensing, while becoming a close friend.

We would like to thank the MIT Sloan School—the fifth floor, the deans, the MIT Leadership Center, and Executive Education—for providing a stimulating environment, resources, and infrastructure for our work. Thanks also goes to the Lean Aerospace Initiative and the Program on the Pharmaceutical Industry for much needed research support. Thanks to all of the staff at MIT Sloan Executive Education for helping to design X-teams into your programs and supporting them magnificently from entry through mentoring to graduation. You have been amazing. Praise also to Joanna Maunder for working with our teams and to INSEAD for providing precious institutional support.

Thanks to the staff at Harvard Business School Press, especially Jeff Kehoe, for advising and moving from manuscript to finished product. It's been a great partnership. And enormous thanks to Lucy McCauley, who helped us to transform the manuscript from academic to practitioner mode, from confusion to clarity. Thanks also to the *Sloan Management Review* and Katrin Kaeufer for helping to create the first X-team article.

Thanks to our brainstorming friends, family, and colleagues for helping us come up with the X-team name and the book title—to Ted, Naomi, and Phil Berk, Amy Edmondson, Bill Isaacs, Jonathan Lehrich, Wanda Orlikowski, Mary Schaefer, Jamil Simon, Jamie Wacks, and to all the members of the Organizational Behavior area at INSEAD.

Finally, thanks to our friends and families for encouraging us despite all the times that we weren't available and weren't in the best of moods. To Deborah's children, Marisa, Anna, Laura, and Bertie, "Mom is not going to write another book anytime soon, promise," and to Henry, "Thanks for making the link between leadership and teams; sometimes it's hard to see what's right in front of you." To Henrik's family, in France (Annie), in Sweden (Karin, Bertil, Martin, Katarina, Mats, Johan, and Erik), and in the United States (Kathy, Big Pete, and Little Pete): "No more book writing over the holidays!"

# When Bad Things Happen to Good Teams

P AUL DAVIDSON had just received permission to work with his team of three engineers on the second version of a software product that promised exciting things for the company.[1] The teammates brought in ten more engineers and vowed that this time they would get to include all the features that they thought customers wanted. Paul had just finished a course in continuous improvement and was anxious to apply his new knowledge. This team would meet its deadlines and learn along the way. After working hard to get an elegant design and prototype, the team put together an overall plan, identifying all the tasks and setting achievable delivery dates. The team members committed to the schedule, agreed on a clear set of goals, and moved into full-scale implementation. Excitement was high. The team knew what it wanted to build and hoped to show top management just how well it could deliver on those specs.

Then, a few months into the schedule, an upper-level manager suggested that the product be changed to meet some needs that customers had raised. Somehow these needs had not been considered by Paul and his team. In this market-driven organization, managers and customers met often. After a very intense user convention, customers had pointed out some features that they thought were essential—and management wanted to show its support of this process. Paul was reluctant to make the changes, saying that the team members were committed to the schedule and they didn't want to do anything to jeopardize meeting their deadlines. They were on a crusade to show that continuous improvement works, and they would meet their schedule no matter what it took. The team members saw the manager as engaging in some kind of power play; the manager felt that the team was inflexible and unresponsive.

When layoffs came, the team lost two members and resentment grew. Paul requested that more people be assigned to the project, but his request was denied. Deadlines slipped, two more team members left, morale dropped, and Paul left the company—feeling that he had no future with such an inhospitable organization. None of the other three original engineers wanted to fill the void, and the team just kept getting further and further behind—while they all circulated their résumés.

How did a team that started off with so much talent and enthusiasm end up failing? Here was a team that considered customer needs and strove for efficiency. Here was a set of people who worked well together, committed to a plan, and were very motivated to make that plan a reality. Here was a group of people who had a lot to offer this organization and wanted to work hard. They were excited and energized, and then it all fell apart for one primary reason: the team was too inwardly focused.

This diagnosis may surprise you, and indeed we will explain shortly how focused, inward-looking teams have traditionally been considered ideal, offering a recipe for success that includes close camaraderie, trust, and a solid process for working well together. But consider how in the case of this software team that inward focus caused it to build a wall between itself and the outside world. The team members came to believe that they had the answers and that anyone who disagreed with them was wrong, and perhaps even had bad motives. They became more and more rigid in their practices and beliefs so that everything was seen with an us-versus-them mind-set. The more negative feedback they received, the more they rebelled against what the company and customers were asking of them. And so a vicious downward spiral ensued.

We have seen many teams fail, or slowly decline, just as Paul Davidson's team did. One such team in the financial services industry had a highly promising product, but because team members failed to get buy-in from division managers, they saw their product slowly starve from lack of resources. Another group in a computer company worked well as a team but did not gather important competitive information. Its product was obsolete before launch.

These stories are doubly sad because they are about good teams made up of talented, committed individuals. These are the kinds of teams led by people whom others admire and whose footprints they have tried to follow. These are teams that seem to be doing everything right—establishing roles and responsibilities, building trust among team members, defining goals—and nevertheless see their projects get axed.

Why do bad things happen to good teams? As we have already begun to explore in our analysis of Paul Davidson's team, teams often fail because their members are following the models and theories that are written up in best-selling books on team effectiveness. It is the view of team performance that we have all learned, the one that we carry in our heads, and the one that dominates executive team training—namely, that all a team needs to succeed is to focus within, on its own process, on the problem at hand, and on each other as team members. This is the mental model that guides our actions when we create teams and set their agendas. And this is the model that feels comfortable to most people who want to be part of a team in which members care about each other and want to get the job done quickly. This is the model that makes us effective at shaping the internal dynamics of teams—how to build team spirit and work around a conference table, how to make rational decisions and allocate work, how to set goals and create roles for individual members.

The problem is that the world has changed and this model of internal focus doesn't work so well anymore. Fierce innovation-driven competition has forced dramatic changes in organizational life. As the competitive wars rage, battles are increasingly being won with the weapons of innovation, speed, and organizational linkages creating synergies that efficiently satisfy customer needs. It is organizational teams that are increasingly called on to lead these battles.

In addition, the world is plagued by complex problems like poverty, global warming, and political violence. These problems can only be addressed when people from diverse sectors like business, government, and nongovernmental organizations (NGOs) work together. It is teams that will ultimately be the major actors in carrying out this important work.

In this new world, leadership can no longer exist only at the top of the organization but must also be distributed throughout the organization and shared with teams. When innovation is king and keeping your finger on the pulse of technology and changing markets is critical, it is no longer the case that someone at the top will figure it all out and everyone else will execute. When organizations are faced with complex problems and resources are dispersed, leadership needs to be distributed across many players, both within and across organizations, up and down the hierarchy—wherever information, expertise, vision, new ways of working together, and commitment reside. Within this world of "distributed leadership" teams cannot look solely inward.[2] Being called to take on a new leadership role, they must become the eyes that read the changing environment, the people who bring commitment and energy to the task, the visionaries who help shape a new future, and the inventors of innovative solutions for business and world problems. Now teams must work with others to create distributed leadership in action as they innovate and create change.

Therefore, the old way of carrying out teamwork that dominates the culture, a way that is largely internally focused (as Paul Davidson's team was), is only half the story. It is the half that teaches us to be effective in shaping the team's internal dynamics. But the other half—managing externally, across team boundaries—gets ignored. And being only half-right, the story can be very wrong. We are not talking "either/or." What is needed is an internal focus combined with an external approach. Evidence now exists suggesting that team success at leading, innovating, and getting things done means managing both inside and outside the team.

## The Other Half of the Story: X-Teams

Consider the Netgen team at Microsoft.[3] This small team was formed when Tammy Savage, a manager in business strategy, realized that Microsoft didn't really know what technologies it needed to develop for thirteen- to twenty-four-year-olds (the "Netgeners," or Internet generation). So she created the Netgen team to get to know these customers better and then to develop software to meet their needs. But selling the idea to the top brass and getting the resources to find ways to understand the Internet generation was not easy. Bill Gates was not that interested—the ideas were too vague and it was not clear what the actual product would be. The team realized it had to make some changes to both its product ideas and its pitch. By the next meeting the team had data about what features Netgeners might like and how Microsoft could benefit from this approach. While Bill Gates was still not that enthusiastic, another top manager gave the team the thumbs-up, and Tammy became a group manager.

The first thing the Netgen team did was to bring together a set of college students and ask them to work on a business plan. The team wasn't interested in the plan itself but rather in seeing how the students used technology as they worked together. After a few weeks, team members understood a lot more about how Netgeners used technology and what they wanted it to do for them. And so began the development and production of "threedegrees," a product that would allow groups of people to do things together online, such as listening to music or creating a joint photo album. Microsoft gave Netgen new space and many new members. Team members got out their PDAs and contacted anyone who might be able to help or provide expertise. They borrowed lots of ideas from others but invented their own unique form of creative development. They looked at their competitors' products and kept top management informed of their progress while aligning with several management demands. They shopped for the best technologies within Microsoft and, when necessary, developed some of their own. They worked through many technical glitches and internal disagreements. And they always kept going back to the customer—the real Netgeners—to test their ideas. Then they produced the code and moved it into Microsoft Messenger, the firm's leading instant messaging application.

The Netgen team offers a case in point that sometimes a small group can create change in a large company. In the end Netgen produced innovative new software ideas and technology for the internet generation. And Tammy Savage is heading up a whole new group that focuses on learning about customer needs and integrating them into product design.

The Netgen team is what we call an "X-team." The *X* in *X-team* underlines the point that an X-team is externally oriented, with members working outside their boundaries as well as inside them. The *X* in *X-team* emphasizes that years of research and practice have shown that while managing internally is necessary, it is managing externally that enables teams to lead, innovate, and succeed in a rapidly changing environment. An X-team differs from a traditional team in three main ways. First, to create effective goals, plans, and designs, members must go outside the team; they must have high levels of *external activity*. As Netgen did by seeking top management support and funding, spending lots of time understanding customer needs before designing its product, and looking around the organization for pockets of expertise that it could build on. X-teams seek out information about the customer (often directly as opposed to secondhand), the technology, the market, and the competition. They figure out what directions top management is moving in and work to either change that direction or link to it. They learn from other teams and adapt to new information. They work hard to coordinate with others and get buy-in from upper levels. They have effective dialogue with many people outside the team.

Second, X-teams combine all of that productive external activity with *extreme execution* inside the team. X-teams develop internal processes that enable members to coordinate their work and execute effectively while simultaneously carrying out external activity. For example, the Netgen team had various members give presentations to top management (external activity), but then team members discussed the feedback they received about those presentations and changed them. Team members showed extreme execution in their ability to learn from their external forays and change going forward. This fine-tuned internal process is also shown in Netgen's ability to get large amounts of information about the customer and translate it into software features that customers wanted.

Third, X-teams incorporate *flexible phases*, shifting their activities over the team's lifetime. Netgen team members first engaged in *exploration*—learning about customer needs, top management expectations, and their own passions about what they wanted to create. Then they moved on to *exploitation*—actually developing the software that customers wanted and competitors did not yet have. Finally, they engaged in *exportation*—transferring their product to another part of Microsoft and learning from their experiences. As with other effective X-teams, Netgen changed its process over time to keep the product moving along and to deal with the demands that different phases of a task presented.

Together, those three elements—external activity, extreme execution, and flexible phases—form the principles by which X-teams guide themselves. But how are they able to actually carry out those principles? What kind of structure supports such teams? The answer largely lies in what we have come to call the three "X-factors." First is *extensive ties* to useful outsiders who enable teams to go beyond their boundaries, coordinate their activities, and adapt over time. For example, Netgen made use of its ties to other people inside and outside the firm and developed new ties along the way. Team members found people with the expertise and information they needed, and after talking to these people, they got the names of others. Second, *expandable tiers* allow teams like Netgen to structure themselves. Tammy and a few other managers composed the core that led the team, a number of other members carried out the work, and other members dropped in for short periods to work on specific pieces of work. Finally, *exchangeable membership* allows a team like Netgen to include members who come in and out of the team and to rotate leadership.

The result is an X-team whose members frequently navigate across the team's boundary. This enables the team to get more information and to adapt quickly to new circumstances. This is an agile group of people who can bring innovation to a company and satisfaction to themselves. This kind of team also creates schedules and plans, goals and commitment, but it does so after working interactively with others to jointly define what the team will do and what the final product will be. Here excitement and satisfaction grow as the team gets positive feedback from successes in an organization that has already offered its input and support.

These new, externally oriented, adaptive X-teams have been able to make great things happen. They consistently outperform traditional teams across a wide variety of functions and industries. One such team in the oil business has done an exceptional job of disseminating information about an innovative method of oil exploration throughout the organization. X-teams in sales have brought in more revenue to a telecommunications company. Drug development X-teams have been more adept at getting external technologies into their companies. Product development X-teams in the computer industry have been more innovative—and have outperformed more traditional teams on time and budget metrics. Consulting X-teams have been better able to serve client needs.

Will every team that is internally focused fail? Should every team be an X-team? The answer is clearly no. X-teams are not needed when team goals and organizational goals are clearly aligned and the team has the support it needs, when team members have all the information they require to get their work done and the information and knowledge they need is not changing rapidly, and when the team's task is not highly interdependent with other work within the organization.

As we've said, however, we do believe that the world has changed and that X-teams are better equipped to deal with the challenges that this new world represents than are traditional teams. Specifically, the shift from a singular reliance on command-and-control leadership to more of a distributed leadership mind-set requires additional dialogue and alignment up and down the organization.[4] X-teams like the Netgen team work with top management to lead the organization. It was Tammy Savage and her team who realized that the Internet generation had to be better understood, who built commitment to this new way of looking at the market, who invented software to meet customer needs, and who pushed top management to have a greater focus on the voice of the customer. It was this X-team that reached out across functional, divisional, and corporate boundaries; challenged corporate assumptions; and provided software ideas and technology that helped Microsoft compete in a changing marketplace.

X-teams have emerged to help firms solve complex problems, adapt to changing conditions, innovate, and gain competitive advantage. Their entrepreneurial focus helps them in getting resources and in seeking and maintaining buy-in from stakeholders. Their links to top management, customers, competitors, and technologies enable them to link top-level strategy with knowledge and ideas from the ground. Their external focus helps them to respond more nimbly than traditional teams to the rapidly changing characteristics of work, technology, and customer demands and to more effectively link their work to other organizational initiatives.

This book is the story of X-teams. It is a story about ordinary people doing extraordinary things simply by shifting to a more external approach. These teams combine extreme execution inside with an interactive approach across the team's boundaries. These teams make use of extensive ties outside the team and the firm and have a structure of expandable tiers that enables members to come in and out of the team, changing their roles as needed. These teams shift their activities over their lifetime as the task demands. In short, these teams are adaptive and flexible. The bulk of this book is about how the strengths of X-teams can be leveraged to orchestrate superior performance and action in an increasingly complex and changing world.

The book contains many examples of specific teams but also examines forward-looking companies that have established specific programs, incentives, and processes to create and maintain X-teams. We will examine how such programs are established, how they are structured, the checklists used to guide team member activity, and the subsequent results of these endeavors. We will focus on the full story—the integration of the internal and external approach to team management—and the organizational context needed to make it all work.

## Who Should Read This Book?

Managers at all levels in any organization in which teams are important will find this book useful. From senior-level executives whose organization's performance depends on the success of its teams, to the team members in the trenches responsible for getting the job done. From those who have to create the conditions and incentives to make teams successful, to those responsible for team member training and development. From the individuals working on large, complex projects involving cutting-edge technologies and hundreds of people, to those working in small groups trying to make ongoing improvements in their work or community.

This book is intended for those people who are searching for the answers to these questions: How can firms move to more decentralized structures and become more innovative? How do we move leadership to lower levels within the firm? How do we get people who are already overwhelmed with day-to-day work to focus on new directions for the future? How do we unleash the creativity of people who want to make a difference and create change but don't know what to do to make it happen? How do we link top-level strategy with new initiatives below? And, at the most basic level, how can we improve the performance and satisfaction in teams that form the core of today's organizations?

We also hope that this book will provide a valuable resource to academics, consultants, or anyone else struggling with the challenges of understanding and managing teams in a new organizational environment. We hope to provide a framework that will reshape some of the fundamental assumptions that permeate the world of small-group research and practice. We hope to shift the research lens from one that rests on the team's boundary and focuses inward, to one that moves inside and outside the team. We hope to shift people's thinking about what a team is, how to build a team, and how to manage team transitions. We hope to shift your ideas about what makes a team effective, and ultimately, how to create innovation and change in organizations.

## Research Approach

The ideas behind the X-team concept emerged from a research program that occurred over many years and featured a number of coauthors. The ideas come from watching real teams discover that taking a more external approach enabled them to succeed. The research includes many different kinds of teams, including nursing teams, sales teams, consulting teams, product development teams, and oil exploration teams. These teams span multiple industries, including telecommunications, education, energy, pharmaceuticals, computers, and financial services. The results have been written up in many journal articles that are referenced here for those readers who would like to see more of the statistics and sampling procedures that provide the basis for this book.

Our earliest study—of nursing teams—examined what happened to teams that had extensive team-building training as part of a large quality of work life project. The hope was that through training in conflict resolution and decision making, nursing team performance could improve. Unfortunately, though much time and money was spent on this project, and nurses reported a greater ability to interact with each other, audit data indicated little change in performance.

Next came a study of one hundred sales teams in the telecommunications industry. Results showed that teams that excelled at internal dynamics were more satisfied than other teams and thought that they were better performers, but also showed no differences in actual revenue attainment than teams that did not have this focus. This raised an important question: what does account for team performance?

By collecting both qualitative and quantitative data, by looking at the logs of team member activity, by interviewing scores of members and leaders in consulting teams, product development teams, drug development teams, and oil exploration teams, answers began to emerge. It was an external emphasis paired with external ties, an expandable structure, a flexible membership, and extreme execution that differentiated high- and low-performing teams. It was also the ability of these teams to shift their activities over their lifetime and not get bogged down in one phase of work.

But these were teams that already existed within organizations. The next question was this: could we *create* such teams? Furthermore, could teams work with top management to *lead* change? Here we moved into consulting and executive education mode and actually intervened in organizations to create X-teams. At Merrill Lynch, BP, and CVRD (the Brazilian mining conglomerate), and within our own institutions, our interventions have been very successful, with teams developing new financial products for Merrill Lynch, designing new processes for project management at BP, formulating a global strategy for CVRD, and consulting to entrepreneurial enterprises around the world. We'll look at some of these teams—and how companies can develop their own X-teams—in the last part of this book.

## About the Book

We have divided this book into three parts. Part 1, chapters 1 and 2, describes the dominant "internal view" and explains how the world has changed in fundamental ways, rendering the old paradigm obsolete. Part 2, chapters 3–6, builds a framework to overcome the challenges. It outlines the building blocks needed for teams to engage in a complex web of complementary internal and external activities. Part 3, chapters 7–9, pulls it all together and explains how managers can make the X-team model work for them.

### Why Good Teams Fail

Before offering a solution, we need to understand the true nature, scope, and depth of the challenge. Thus, we begin this book with a journey through the landscape of existing thinking on teams. Chapter 1 describes the view of team effectiveness that we have all learned, the one we carry with us in our heads and execute daily, the one that has always made the most sense to us. We then begin looking at the evidence showing that this dominant view does not work anymore.

In chapter 2 we explain why the old model does not work. The reason? Driven by increasingly fierce, fast, and innovation-based competition, organizational life has changed in a number of fundamental ways. First, organizational structures are loose, spread-out systems with numerous alliances rather than multilevel centralized hierarchies. Second, organizations are dependent on information that is complex, externally dispersed, and rapidly changing. Third, teams' tasks are increasingly interwoven with other tasks both inside and outside the organization. As a consequence of these changes in organizational life, distributed leadership is now part of the corporate landscape. All of these changes have had a profound impact on teams' job descriptions; in fact, they have fundamentally changed the rules of the game. We explain how.

### What Works

To deal with the new realities, teams need to engage in a range of external activities. This is the first core principle of X-teams and the subject of chapter 3. First, *scouting* helps a team gather information located throughout the company and the industry. It involves searches inside and outside the organization to understand who has knowledge and expertise. It also means investigating markets, new technologies, competitor activities, and organizational cultures. Second, *ambassadorship* is aimed at managing upward—that is, marketing the project and the team to the company power structure, maintaining the team's reputation, lobbying for resources, and managing allies and adversaries. Third, *task coordination* is for managing the lateral connections across functions and the interdependencies with other units. Team members negotiate with other groups, trade their services, and get feedback on how well their work meets expectations.[5]

As chapter 4 concretely lays out, internal processes are also needed to complement the external ones. The second core principle of X-teams, extreme execution, contains the internal processes that are needed to seamlessly coordinate external processes of an X-team, hold the team together, and enable the team to integrate information and expertise. By using the term *extreme* we mean to underline the fact that external activity does not eliminate the need for internal process; rather, it expands that need. External activity brings additional information, divergent opinions, and political bickering into the team. Extreme execution is needed to keep the team moving in the face of these additional challenges.

Chapter 5 describes the third core principle of X-teams: flexible phases. This is a model consisting of three stages—exploration, exploitation, and exportation—as illustrated by the story of a team at Merrill Lynch.[6] This chapter is a critical part of the X-team story because it lays out how team activities need to shift over time to maintain innovation and speed. It is also a central part of the book since it shows how these shifts over time become a vehicle through which the X-team demonstrates distributed leadership in action. The second part of the book concludes with chapter 6, outlining the three X-factors (as illustrated by the Netgen story)—extensive ties, expandable tiers, and exchangeable membership—which are the structural components that support the three core principles of X-teams.

### How to Build Effective X-Teams

In the final part we pull everything together that the book has described so far and offer a hands-on guide to creating X-teams. In chapter 7 we provide concrete steps and checklists so that teams can move from a more traditional form to an X-team approach. Chapter 8 then describes in detail how to launch and manage X-team programs. Here we build on our experiences at Merrill Lynch, BP, CVRD, and MIT, where we, with the help of others, have successfully built a series of X-teams and a structure of ongoing innovation and organizational change.

Chapter 9, our final chapter, outlines how top management can build an organization in which X-teams thrive. Here we show how three successful organizations—Southwest Airlines, Oxfam, and Procter & Gamble—use X-teams as a vehicle for distributed leadership in action. We articulate the key dimensions of distributed leadership, show how X-teams can embody and give life to this form of leadership, and outline what top management can do to foster such an organization. After all, X-teams cannot meet their full potential to lead without a supportive organizational context. While building such a context only happens over a long period, and with a lot of work, organizations need to foster the processes, structures, and culture necessary to unlock the potential of X-teams. In turn, X-teams help model and shape these processes, structures, and culture.

Teams, teams, teams. They take up enormous amounts of our time, frustrate us, compel us, and motivate us to get the job done. We are sometimes told that teams are out of vogue, yet companies are filled with teams and still struggling with how to improve their performance, pundits are still writing books on how to manage them, and we are all living with them at home and at work. We are surrounded by teams and yet they remain an enigma.

We believe not only that teams are here to stay but also that their importance as vehicles for leadership, innovation, and change is likely to increase. As a consequence, the challenges they face are likely to become ever more multifaceted and difficult. This book offers the X-team as the modus operandi to take on these challenges and turn them into breakthrough performance.

Throughout this book we will be looking at a set of teams to help us illustrate the many facets of X-teams. Their stories, some with disguised names, will be woven throughout.

The Southeast and Northwest teams are names given to two consulting teams run by managers we call Sam and Ned. These teams were created in a new organizational design to better serve the educational curriculum needs in particular geographic regions. The teams had to consult on new educational materials and methods that the regions might use. While both teams were created at the same time, with the same mission, and with two very talented leaders, one ended up doing very well—the X-team—and the other ended up imploding.

The Big Bank team demonstrates how an X-team may be critical for new teams that are set up when there is a major organizational change. Here teams in a large telecommunications firm we call BellCo were created to serve industry segments rather than geographic areas. The Big Bank team was put in charge of the banking industry. Team members had to learn how to be more aggressive in their selling, how to cater their sales to this particular customer segment, and how to bundle their existing products into systems that produced a solution for their customer's business issues. On top of that they needed to create new ways to work together and to work with other parts of the organization with whom they were interdependent. In the end, they made it all work and helped the company figure out how their new design could actually be implemented.

The Razr team at Motorola is an example of how an X-team can create radical change in a stodgy culture. Given the challenge of creating a new mobile phone, this team was able to stay true to its name and develop a thin, sleek phone that blew the competition out of the water. Team members were able to do this quickly and despite many political land mines, pockets of resistance, and bureaucracy.

Team Fox demonstrates how one X-team was able to operate in the network-like realm of pharmaceutical companies. Here the core technology of the firm—molecules—come from outside, not inside, the company. Teams need to scout various environments—from universities, to small start-ups, to research labs—to find the molecule they need and figure out how to bring it into a large corporation.

The Netgen team in Microsoft featured near the beginning of this introduction did not start off with top management's blessing. Members had to fight to get resources and to have their ideas heard. They developed a vision and stayed true to that vision even when others in the company ostracized them or grew jealous of their status. They fought to separate from the firm to develop very innovative ideas and then struggled to integrate back into the mainstream of the company. In the end, they managed to merge their ideas into the Microsoft culture.

Before we can explore the lofty results of X-teams like those just described, however, let us begin with the basics: an in-depth look at the existing thinking about teams—and evidence for how that thinking is failing to help organizations meet current challenges.

# PART I

# Why Good
# Teams Fail

# ONE

# Into a Downward Spiral

## *How Our Old Models Lead to Failure*

W HEN TEACHING EXECUTIVE PROGRAMS on teams, we often start the session by asking participants, "What do you think is most important for creating successful teams?" Without much prompting the answers pour out: clear roles and goals, managing conflict, trust, team spirit, rational decision making, keeping the team on track, focused meetings, accountability, allocating work to the right people, rewards for teamwork. The list goes on and on.

While lists differ somewhat from one session to the next, the pattern of responses is clear. The major message is that team members need to support each other and figure out how to work together. They need to set goals and figure out a structure and way of working together to meet those goals. The participants in our sessions aren't slouches. They've done their homework, and their answers mirror the top-selling books and management guru views of what makes a team effective. In one best seller, for example, the authors argue that teams can be high performing to the extent that "they are a small number of people with complementary skills who are equally committed to a common purpose, goals, and working approach for which they hold themselves mutually accountable, and who are deeply committed to one another's personal growth and success."[1]

The key message that is drilled into all of us in team-building sessions and training guides—and what we're all used to practicing in our organizations—is that effective performance depends on *what goes on inside the team.* The camera lens sits on the team boundary and looks inward. Here team members try to figure out what the task is, who they are, and how they will work together to get the job done.[2] This is the basic model of teams that most of us carry in our heads. It is the model that guides our behavior in choosing team members and setting up their basic modes of work.

What's more, this inward orientation comes most naturally to us in a team setting. Teams by their very nature seem to create anxiety in individual members and therefore a focus on the team itself: Will I be liked and accepted by the other members? Can we get the job done with these people? Will we get along? How will we coordinate our efforts? Can we finish the work on time?[3] These are questions that haunt all of us as we enter teams, and we want answers as soon as possible. And so to deal with this anxiety and these questions, team leaders and members try to find areas of agreement, ways to coordinate, goals to achieve, and a sense of camaraderie, accomplishment, and hope early in the process. That's how team members find an identity and sense of belonging, as well as a direction that calms their anxiety and focuses their activity.

These are good things. Good internal team functioning is important for success, so it isn't wrong or surprising that teams focus inward. The problem is that it isn't enough. And, in fact, an exclusively internal focus can be dangerous for teams and their goals.

An inward focus, then, is only half the story when it comes to high-functioning, successful teams. The crucial other half is about the external work of teams—the *X* of the *X-teams* of our book title. This is the half that stresses managing upward and outward, outside the team's boundary as well as inside it. This is the half that looks at the role of the team not solely as a setting for teamwork but also as an agent for innovation and a vehicle for organizational leadership in action. For this role, people need to monitor, market, and manage across the team boundary as well as engage members and build strong ties and processes within the team. But how do we know this is true?

## The Half-Done Hospital Team and Other Unfinished Business

Doubts about the internal model of teams started back in the late 1970s in a quality of work life project in a major New York hospital.[4] One part of the project focused on improving the satisfaction and performance of nursing teams. Turnover and conflicts in the teams were high. Enter a consulting firm. The consultant concentrated on training team members in skills such as problem solving, communication, supervision, group decision making, and conflict resolution.

A lot of time and energy went into the training. The consultant emphasized the importance of understanding teammates' feelings and viewpoints and coming to consensus on what the team really wanted to achieve. During the course of the project, the unit did improve communication and increase problem-solving capabilities. People felt more pride in their work, individuals learned interpersonal skills, and the number of work conflicts decreased. Unfortunately, after spending thousands of dollars and many hours of time, the consensus was that these changes would be short lived. Furthermore, it became clear from nursing audit data that there was little clear proof of any improvements in the performance of the nursing teams because of these interventions.[5] And even though the hospital sponsored many other projects in this quality of work life improvement program, team performance did not change.

More proof that internal process was not enough came in a study of a hundred sales teams in the telecommunications industry. Here the focus was on whether teams with effective internal processes performed better. These were teams that followed the guidance of best-selling texts and had clear roles and goals, practiced open communication, considered how best to weigh individual input, and supported one another. The results showed that though such teams' members were more satisfied, and though they thought themselves to be high performers, it was not internal processes that differentiated high- and low-performing teams. In short, team performance, as measured by revenue attained by the team, could not be predicted in any way by looking solely at how members interacted with one another. The old model that we all believe in simply did not tell the whole story; it was not enough.[6]

And then a study of forty-five product development teams in the high-tech arena started to answer the question of what *did* affect performance.[7] Teams that scouted out new ideas from outside their boundaries, received feedback from and coordinated with outsiders, and got support from top managers were able to build more innovative products faster than those that dedicated themselves solely to efficiency and working well together.

Still more support came from studies of consulting teams and pharmaceutical teams. The consulting teams that were more externally focused performed better in terms of client satisfaction and ratings of top management than did teams that focused only on their internal interaction. It's interesting to note that although teams that were primarily internally focused were more satisfied and performed well during their early months, over time both satisfaction and performance fell. The pharmaceutical teams that were externally focused were better able to identify usable molecules and evaluate those molecules' potential for the company than were teams that focused on their own knowledge base.[8]

By now, other team studies have replicated these results.[9] When a team task requires information, cooperation, resources, support, and expertise from outside its boundaries, then a sole focus on internal interactions is simply not enough. When adaptation in response to changing external conditions or working with top management to implement a new strategy is needed, an exclusive internal focus can be lethal. When success depends on keeping up with technology, markets, competitors, and other external stakeholders, then some external focus is essential.

And yet, despite twenty years of research to the contrary, it is the internal models that remain lodged in our brains and our actions. In executive sessions we hear again and again that team performance pivots around exclusively internal processes. In fact, when we are starting a team, it is that internal focus that takes over—even though we know that the data tells a different story. The numbers that support external activities in addition to internal ones are there in black and white and have been for some time, but they have been largely ignored.

Why does the old model linger? Perhaps because it remains tacit and unexamined. We do not question it and so continue to believe in it. Or perhaps there is some evolutionary value to an internal focus. Early humans probably survived more easily if they stayed in groups that developed trust and worked efficiently together. Perhaps these ancestors found an identity in their group, which gave them a drive to survive, to fight with and for each other in the face of adversity. Inward-looking groups could protect themselves more than individuals could, and so this propensity has been passed along to us when we set up our teams. Furthermore, if the world at that time was reasonably stable—technology was not rapidly changing, threats were constant but predictable, the activities of securing food and shelter were ongoing and repetitive tasks—then external activity was not crucial for survival. In fact, external exploration was probably fraught with danger. In such a world, why threaten internal security and cohesion by going outside? Or perhaps, more simply, the old model lingers because our individual and collective need for safety and identity outweigh all other considerations.

For whatever reasons, an exclusive internal focus is clearly no longer the recipe for survival and success. Rather, the solution to this problem is to add a more active role in relating to people outside the team's boundaries. But first, let's delve more deeply into what happens in these exclusively internally focused teams to set them on such a misguided path—and keep them moving in the wrong direction.

## A Tale of Two Teams

The road to dissolution is not straight or quick. Rather, things often seem to be fine at the start and then slowly unravel. Of course, each team evolves in its own unique way, but nonetheless, some patterns for fully internally focused teams seem to emerge. To explore these patterns, let's compare two consulting teams from their formation through to the ultimate dissolution of one team. Both teams were newly formed and their task was to consult to school districts in a particular geographic area, so we will call them the Southeast and Northwest teams, with leaders Sam and Ned, respectively. The teams were created as part of a new strategy developed by the organization's president to improve consulting services to geographic regions. The Southeast team followed an exclusively internal focus; the Northwest team melded the internal and external in a much more integrated way. The Southeast team saw itself as a team set up to satisfy its members and complete a task. The Northwest team saw itself as a change agent working with top management to create innovative new solutions for district problems. Thus, there was a different orientation right from the start.

Why Sam chose to focus inward and Ned chose to move externally as well, to be part of a larger organizational change, is not entirely clear. What's clear from our work with many teams over the years is that some teams in almost every organization do take on this more integrated approach and that some leaders set their teams up to engage in external, as well as internal, activity. These are the teams that have outperformed others. These are the teams that have provided us with the lessons in this book. The stories of the Southeast and Northwest teams show how little decisions made at the beginning can set the stage for how teams will evolve over their life spans. Specifically, the integrated approach enables both greater internal satisfaction in the long run and better external adaptation and performance.

In interviews before the teams even had their first meetings, Sam and Ned communicated very different strategies for how they wanted their teams to operate. Sam was concerned that team members might be uncomfortable with the new organizational structure, and he wanted to give them time to get to know each other and to figure out the work that they needed to do. After this team-building period, he intended to get more active in the districts and explain all the wonderful things that the team could do for them. But first he wanted the team to be a safe haven in the midst of change. Ned, too, wanted to build a strong, cohesive team, but he also wanted team members to get out into the districts right away. He thought that the team needed to start by diagnosing the districts' various needs and then experiment with solutions. These different strategies set the teams on different paths that would never converge.

### *Two Teams, Two Strategies*

When first interviewed, Sam underscored his internally focused strategy—his desire for the Southeast members to come together as a team and study material about their districts. He saw his role as that of a facilitator and support to the team as people learned about each other and shared the information that each had about the districts. He said that somewhere along the line they were going to need a lot of exchange with the districts, but he viewed this activity as secondary to building the team, figuring out how members would work together, and sharing existing information about the districts.

Ned differed from Sam in wanting a more integrated strategy for his Northwest team—to get first-hand information about the districts and to get out there right away. His rationale for this approach was twofold:

first, to see the districts and their needs with new eyes (as members of this newly formed team, not from the vantage of their other jobs) and, second, to build credibility with the people in the districts who would have to sign off on the new approach. And he saw his role as the primary proponent of this new approach with the districts' local leadership, superintendents, and principals.

Ned was quite articulate in his interviews about seeing the districts in a new way and learning what they really wanted so that the team could meet those needs and gain credibility. He argued, "Even though I have knowledge about every district up there, I have been looking at them from one point of view. We all need to broaden our perspective and see what the districts see their needs to be. The first task is to get them to express their needs for services. We need to customize our services to these people: this is what we can bring you; tell us what your needs are, and we will design something to address those. If we do not do this, we lose our credibility."[10]

From the outset, then, Sam and Ned envisioned different strategies for their teams. Sam had a primary goal of creating an enthusiastic team with open communication. Initially, the level of interaction with the region would be low; only at some undefined point in the future did he envision a lot of interaction with the field. Even when Sam discussed interacting with the region, he referred to the data the team members already had, rather than that from primary sources and newly collected information. What's more, communication would go one way—with the team letting the region know what it was going to do.

Contrast that strategy against Ned's, whose primary goal was to improve service to the regions as outlined by the president. Ned was much more in line with the strategic goal of the new organizational design—he and his team would be the ones to figure out how to make the new strategy a reality. He anticipated high levels of two-way communication with the regions intended to broaden the perspective of team members, to diagnose the region's needs, to obtain feedback on team ideas, and to sell the team's services to the customer. Ned did not believe that his team members had all the data they needed to serve the region. Furthermore, he believed that his team saw the information it did have through old lenses. He planned to promote a new mind-set through an interactive approach: hearing the needs of the region and then testing whether the team's plans met those needs. And yet his strategy was not focused exclusively externally. He planned many team meetings for members to share what they learned in their forays into the regions and to create plans to match the organization's new strategy. While these meetings helped pull the team together, it did put a strain on members as they tried to juggle their jobs *and* their teamwork.

Thus, the internal and integrated approaches differed in terms of primary goals—get to know how to work as a team or get to know the external environment. They also differed in their amount of external interaction (low or high) and their methods of information gathering (i.e., use existing member knowledge or seek new information from outsiders). The type of interaction with the environment also differed between the two approaches, with one informing the region of the team's intentions and decisions and the other actively probing and getting feedback from those outside the team. The teams differed further in terms of whether they approached their regions as they had before or whether they opted to see the regions from a new perspective. Finally, the teams differed in terms of whether they worked to excel as a team or whether they worked to help top management lead the way to a new form of interaction with the districts (see table 1-1).

Note, however, that both team leaders wanted to create cohesive teams and both wanted to get organized and move quickly to get the job done. But one team leader decided on team building as the primary goal, with knowledge about the outside built on existing information and mind-sets. The other organized to first go out with new eyes and then set goals

**TABLE 1-1**

## The internal versus the integrated approach

| | Sam's "internal" team (Southeast) | Ned's "integrated" team (Northwest) |
|---|---|---|
| **Primary goal** | Create an enthusiastic team | Understand the needs of the external regions |
| **Secondary goal** | Inform the region of what the team has decided | Create team cohesion and organization |
| **Team building** | Come together as a team by learning about each other and sharing knowledge | Come together as a team while learning about the region |
| **Initial amount of interaction with the environment** | Low | High |
| **Source of information used to map the environment/task** | Inside team; old, secondary sources | Outside team; new, primary sources |
| **Type of interaction with the environment** | One way: inform | Two way: diagnose/feedback/invent |
| **Overall focus** | Build a team | Help the organization implement a new strategy |

for the district—team building was to be a result of this external activity. The point is that both the internal and external activities must happen— but small differences in emphasis and focus at the very start end up making a big difference later. Sam's approach creates a solution that resists change as it pulls members together around a solution. Ned's approach opens the team up to other viewpoints and dialogue before setting a solution and pulls members together around a process of discovery.

In the short term, the Southeast team members were more satisfied, felt like more of a team, and thought they were making progress on the task. The Northwest team members felt more confused, like less of a team, and unsure about what they were doing together as a team. So the internal focus does help people feel safe, directed, and satisfied with their progress. But over the long term, this early satisfaction turns on itself—and performance suffers.

True to their intentions, each of the teams followed through on the initial strategies their leaders articulated. Of the five consulting teams that one of us studied in this organization, Sam's team had the least interaction with its region and with the top management team. While a lot of time was spent early on trying to define goals and roles, as time went on, many team members missed meetings and enthusiasm declined. In contrast, Ned's team had high levels of interaction with both the region and the top management team. Team meetings were a bit confused at first but improved over time through a lot of work on Ned's part. This integrated team sacrificed some internal cohesion early in its existence for greater understanding of its external world, while the other team sacrificed understanding its external world for greater internal cohesion. And this was the wrong choice.

### The Vicious Downward Spiral

By the end of a year, the top management team, the superintendents in the regions, and team members themselves were surveyed—and the Southeast team scored the lowest. The Northwest team, on the other hand, was one of the top performers.

Why does an exclusively internal focus have such negative results? Why do a few different steps at the start lead you over a cliff as opposed to the next campsite? Why does a sole focus within disable your ability to see and act and gain acceptance outside? Why does initial activity aimed externally hamper your early progress as a team but end up helping in the long run? The exclusive internal focus poses numerous problems that together become a vicious downward spiral (see figure 1-1).

FIGURE 1-1

## The vicious downward spiral

- Team members are unable to diagnose and update existing views of the needs and expectations of external stakeholders, including management and customers.

- The team does not establish relationships with outsiders, and so others do not feel part of the process.

*Starting from behind*

- Members are unable to move beyond the initial problem definition and existing knowledge of other members.

- They cannot link the team's work to the organization's goals.

*Stuck on the old: Missing the new*

- Team members miss new trends and major shifts in technology, markets, competition, and the organization.

- They do not have allies in other parts of the organization or outside it.

- They miss the ability to learn best practices and borrow new ideas from others.

- Others in the organization realize that team members are unable to meet outside expectations or chart a new direction for change.

- The team develops a reputation as a losing team, which spreads throughout the organization.

- There are no allies in the organization to block these perceptions.

*The organization as an echo chamber*

*Blaming the enemy out there*

- In the face of opposition, team members begin to see people outside the team as the enemy that does not appreciate or understand them.

- All of the negative perceptions about the team coupled with poor performance push the team into failure mode.

- Members blame each other as well as the "unfair" outside world.

*Failure—inside and out*

Let's look at each phase of the vicious spiral in turn.

*1. Starting from behind.* On the plus side, members of the Southeast team were able to get to know each other quite well and pull together a lot of information about the regions. They even had a head start on thinking about what they might do in the regions. The trouble was that they did not do a good job on the latter. Team members found that they couldn't effectively diagnose the needs of the region or of top management. Since they did not often venture beyond their own team boundaries, they did not really know what superintendents wanted and so could not create highly valued interventions. They also had a hard time determining management's expectations, formulating team goals that were congruent with organizational goals, and communicating with top management. Without information from the regions and upper levels, team members did not even fully understand their task. To compound the problem, top management was implementing a new organizational design that required consultants to create new approaches for their districts. Working from their old mental models of the districts and their jobs, and sharing old information, this team's members were left behind from the start—unable to move to a new way of thinking and operating.

None of this means Sam and his team were stupid. They made a common mistake: their desire to bond and help each other through this difficult new task made them focus inward. While that focus helped them understand each other's viewpoints and a sense of the task, it didn't help them see how their viewpoints might be incomplete or outdated. And they did not bond with any outsiders with a vested interest in helping or correcting those views. If anything, the internal bonding made their boundary even thicker, and they became less motivated to leave their safe haven. And so the mistakes were amplified.

In contrast, the Northwest team members rated themselves as having a high ability to predict regional needs because of high levels of interaction with those regions. Meeting notes showed that this team was closest to the pulse of current issues in the region and in the organization. Team members were asked to report on important events in the districts so that everyone knew what was going on. This sharing of information from the field also helped team members get to know each other and feel like a team meeting a tough challenge. Ned's team was also involved with top management and helped the president design some of the organization-wide regional interventions. When the president had to miss a meeting, Ned was asked to chair it.

Ned's initial decision to send members outside kept them from coming up with solutions quickly and caused stress all around. Like other teams, they wanted the answer sooner rather than later. Ned dealt with that stress, however, by providing the team with a focused task: understand the context in which you operate first. This one decision helped members realize that they did not have all the answers and that others saw the situation differently. It expanded their view of the situation, allowed them to update outdated views, and gave them a better sense of what was going on in the moment.

Once they had a more accurate view of the situation, they could invent ways to improve what was going on in the regions. Furthermore, while they were diagnosing their situation and the needs and expectations of those around them, they were building relationships with key stakeholders—people who would then be more apt to help them in the future and keep them on course. Essentially, they set the stage for dialogue with the outside world. The price they paid was lower team cohesion and higher levels of confusion early on about what their final product would be. So while Sam could have done better by being more externally active in this early stage, Ned struggled with finding the time to do external work while simultaneously helping his team members bond and understand that their early confusion would yield better answers in the long run.

*2. Stuck on the old: Missing the new.* Since Sam's team members relied on existing viewpoints and dated information to understand their region and the top management team, they missed critical changes. Their region was looking for new types of curricula, but the team members never understood the shift in style. Top management was trying to get team members to move away from their professional specialties and act as generalists to the region—but this message never made it to the team. Top management also asked the teams to put together regional profiles, but without new information, the Southeast team did a poor job. In short, Sam's team operated with a very old map of the situation, leaving its members out of step with the very people they needed to satisfy. All their actions were reactive rather than proactive. They were working hard but couldn't seem to get the right answers, and they didn't know why. Thus the vicious spiral began. The initial problem of using dated information and an old mind-set was amplified by poor performance.

Ned's team, on the other hand, picked up on key trends and designed innovative programs to meet the new needs in its region. The region needed a better way to judge how well a school was doing, so the team created a school evaluation project. In meetings Ned asked members to put their specialist hats aside and act as generalists in diagnosing regional needs and brainstorming solutions. All of this was a result of Ned's pushing his team members to look with new eyes at the regions and to respond to the president's desire to create some innovative programs. Here a positive, or virtuous, spiral builds with good ideas spurring positive results as well as positive feelings inside and outside the team.

*3. The organization as an echo chamber.* At an official team leader meeting about three months after the teams were launched, leaders were asked to report on their progress. Since Sam's team members had not been active in the region, had not done a good job on their regional profiles, and had not understood what was expected of them, they were labeled as a "problem team." Soon word spread, and everyone was talking about Sam's problems. Now the team was really in trouble—not only had it received a bad evaluation, but it now had a bad reputation within the organization. Suddenly, other parts of the organization were not as responsive. What might have started as some small blunders at the start of the team's life were amplified as gossip flew through the organization and turned whispers into roars of "problem team."

In contrast, Ned talked about the advances that his team had made on the school evaluation project. The president saw this as a good example of initiation in the field and a way to bring his new strategy to life. He held Ned's team up as an example to follow. Now the team was really flying high. Members had great pride in knowing that they had come up with an idea that others were being encouraged to follow. Other parts of the organization approached team members to learn more about what they were doing and to offer ideas and suggestions. Ned's team was suddenly the one to watch.

*4. Blaming the enemy out there.* As news of the Southeast team's failures spread, team members became dispirited. Looking for someone to blame other than themselves, they focused on the bad guys "out there." For example, Sam told his team that the head of the organization constrained team activity and that team leader meetings were a complete waste of time. Team members began to blame top management and a nonresponsive region for all their problems. Needless to say, relations between the team and its key external stakeholders only continued to decline. The vicious spiral was moving quickly downward.

Ned's team heard a lot of the negative things Sam's team was expressing. They also heard that the president wanted team members to report on promising practices in their region. But since Ned told his team that he did not want them to complain or resist as some other teams were doing, and since team member ideas were brought directly to the president and merited positive feedback, team members began to see the whole change effort and the president more positively. Here the virtuous spiral was getting stronger. Team members used their new knowledge about the region and top management to come up with solutions that worked, they were complimented, word spread, and they started to bond around their newfound success. They were partners with top management in leading the organization in a new direction. This spiral built on itself in a positive direction.

*5. Failure—inside and out.* Once the Southeast team had developed a bad reputation and members refused top management's offer to coach them, the situation just went from bad to worse. Negative initial impressions were cast in concrete. After five months, Sam responded to complaints by saying that the team needed to "develop a plan of action—how can we address the specific needs the department wants to accomplish, get team members to act as ambassadors to the field, and expand the role of school visits?" That agenda approximated the agendas that other teams had had months earlier, but it was too late. Team members sat in judgment of management, and management dismissed the team's attempts to change. Furthermore, new data was interpreted to fit the negative early impressions, making it impossible for the Southeast team to recover. With all of this negative evaluation, members of Sam's team started to blame him and each other so that even internal relations went sour. One year after the teams were formed, the Southeast team still had a negative reputation despite efforts to change. The team eventually disbanded.

The Northwest team was evaluated as having done a "super job" after the first year. Team members felt that the team experience had stretched their abilities and that they had all developed in-depth knowledge of the region. They also felt as if their ideas had been listened to and they had been able to create some interesting and exciting programs in the region. The positive work and positive feedback from outsiders fed on itself, propelling the team to work harder and do more. It was only a year into the program that team members reported beginning to really feel like a team, but their satisfaction with the team had been growing over time. Members also felt as if they had a better overall view of the organization and what it takes to make change happen.

While this chapter has focused on one internally oriented team, we have seen many teams fall into this vicious spiral. Not one of those team leaders was stupid or evil. They usually began with the best of intentions. They wanted to create a highly motivated team that would perform well. They wanted to cultivate a nurturing environment in which team members got along. Early meetings usually showed high energy as members got to know each other, pooled information, set goals, and got to work on the task at hand. And sometimes they were lucky and set the right goals, identified the correct task, and understood the key needs of customers and management. But more often they enthusiastically moved into a negative vicious spiral without even knowing it.

Often these teams do not realize that in creating tight boundaries to make them feel safe, they are simultaneously making it more difficult to step outside those boundaries to see what else exists. They do not realize that by moving quickly to define the task and goals and providing momentum and a sense of accomplishment for their members, they forget to check on whether important stakeholders share those goals and never pull these outsiders into the process. There is no buy-in or support. They do not see that in sharing existing information they may develop trust and that they may be building their interventions and output on dated views and information that no longer represents current reality. By developing their own language, symbols, activities, and T-shirts, they are building cohesion within the team but a less welcoming environment for outsiders. While each step they take may build internal cohesion, they ignore the outside world at their peril—setting off a vicious spiral that results in lower performance and ultimately a dampening of the very cohesion they tried to create.

On the other hand, teams can clearly err on the other side. If a team is too externally oriented, then members may not even feel like part of a team. Their loyalty may be to outside groups and not to the team. Then members have no sense of cohesion or shared identity. They may be unable to stand together and argue for what they think is right. In fact, there is no team in this scenario, only a set of individuals loosely tied together in name and unable to work together effectively. Such a team's members will likely leave at any hint of trouble, happier to abandon ship than to work through the problem. Clay Alderfer, an organizational scholar, calls these two pathologies "overbounded" and "underbounded" teams, respectively.[11]

It is worth noting that the old model—internally focused and self-reflective—works very well for groups that do not need to rely on the external environment in which they function. It works very well in teams that have all the information they need within their borders and those that do not have to work with other groups within the organization. It is a model that works when the task is absolutely clear and not changing and when there is already support within the organization. It works when all the necessary resources are within the team and when changes in technology, markets, and strategy are not relevant.

Unfortunately, as we will examine more closely in the next chapter, the world looks less and less like this every day. The good news is that with a few carefully chosen steps, a team can move from a total internal focus to a more integrated one. What's more, a team can move from acting alone to satisfy members to working with others as part of a distributed leadership effort that engages top management and multiple teams in creating new, innovative solutions and in improving organizational performance. Such a team can escape from a vicious spiral and turn it into a virtuous one.

# TWO

# A Changing World

## *New Kinds of Organizations,*
## *New Kinds of Teams*

Walk into many businesses today and you'll see an organization that resembles neither the hierarchical behemoths of a decade ago nor the companies in which the "organization man" of the 1950s worked.[1] Instead of organizational charts with arrows pointing from the boss's name down to row upon row of reportees, today the lines may radiate out horizontally or circularly, illustrating cooperative rather than linear reporting relationships. Even the look and feel of companies, from software firms to banks to small businesses, has loosened up. The boss's corner office might now house a communal room with sofas and tables where small groups collaborate; her designated parking spot has transformed into a picnic area for lunchtime brainstorming sessions.

Similarly, where there was once a strict hierarchy to make decisions leadership has been pushed down. Meanwhile, middle management is vanishing. There's still an executive level that crafts strategy and vision, but people at the operational level are being asked to take on a whole new brand of responsibility—including strategic leadership. Centralized organizations have given way to loose organizations and decentralized networks. Critical knowledge and information that used to flow vertically from the top is now flowing not only both ways but also laterally across units and organizations. Tasks that used to be designed and executed in clearly delineated silos now span multiple functions and product areas.

What brought about this sea change in companies today? Necessity, as they say, is the mother of invention. Competition has become increasingly fierce, in part because growth has ground to a virtual halt throughout many markets. The time has passed when firms could coast along with a burgeoning market, leaving plenty of room for everyone to grow. Today, growth is reliant on innovation, and competitive survival hinges on new products and ideas. What's more, an increasing number of nimble players continue to enter the arena. New information technologies that lower communication costs allow emerging nations (notice India's new prominence as an IT empire) and smaller firms to enter markets with greater speed, less capital, and more knowledge than ever before.[2]

In this new environment, firms are facing three core challenges: to be entrepreneurial; to track and act on critical knowledge that is complex, specialized, dynamic, and dispersed; and to coordinate and create synergies across increasingly complex, interdependent, and fast-moving tasks.

Our point, of course, is that teams are increasingly put on the hot seat to deal with all of these challenges. In fact, the shifts we have been describing are precisely what make X-teams necessary. But what, exactly, are teams being asked to do? First, as competitive battles are increasingly won in the arena of innovation—and innovation happens at the operational level, not at the executive level—it has fallen to teams to provide the vision, creativity, and entrepreneurship needed to come up with new ideas and to link them to the strategies at the executive level. In effect, teams are now seen as partners with top management in this leadership task of meshing new strategic directives with innovative new products and solutions. This activity requires high levels of interaction up, down, and across the firm. X-teams play a key role in practicing this leadership across levels—and a central part of what we refer to as "distributed leadership."

Second, the space of critical knowledge is ever expanding, becoming more complex, differentiated, and fast changing. To stay ahead in the new competitive environment, firms must be on the leading edge of knowledge in multiple areas simultaneously. This can only be accomplished at the operational level. Therefore, teams must be increasingly responsible for understanding what the current technical, market, cultural, and competitive situation is and where expertise and information can be found. They are increasingly becoming the organization's interpreters of the environment.

Third, in the new competitive environment, firms are under more and more pressure to pursue synergies in their product and service offerings. They are increasingly turning to a strategy of bundling offerings across products and of pursuing cost savings by working on similar platforms across products. Teams are being called on to carry out the organization's necessary but increasingly complex coordination activities resulting from these new strategic imperatives.

None of these new challenges for teams, however, operates—or can be resolved—in isolation. These challenges are interdependent. The relationships between them are not simple and causal, but rather complex and dynamic. The effect on the work of teams and organizations, however, is simply this: it has become much more difficult to do.

The new fierce, innovation-based competition has forced radical changes in the context in which teams must manage the challenges they're now being asked to tackle: specifically, changes in the organizational structures in which teams operate, in the structure of knowledge with which they work, and in the structure of tasks they perform. Simply put, the dominant internal focus described in the previous chapter may have been sufficient in the old tight structure of the command-and-control company working with stable knowledge structures and clearly partitioned tasks. In the new loose, distributed organization, it is not.[3] Recent changes render the internal focus incomplete. Today, teams need to find ways to proactively engage the external environment as well and to exert bold organizational leadership.

To begin to understand why teams need to do this, let's look at a few examples of teams working in the new organizational structure, followed by an examination of the attendant changes in the structures of knowledge and tasks with which these teams must work.

## A New Order

By the start of the twenty-first century, Motorola, the communications industry juggernaut, had fallen off track. The former cell phone industry trailblazer was now lagging behind the more nimble Scandinavian companies, like Ericsson and Nokia, and even Korean players, like Samsung and LG. The problem was that, like many of its historically successful peers, Motorola had grown into a giant and had become, as Yankee Group analyst John Jackson put it, "the stodgy, engineering-driven, Midwestern company that was Motorola."[4] Meanwhile, the competition had become exponentially smarter and more aggressive.

To break out of its stodginess and boost innovation, the company decided to try what many other businesses around it were doing: it loosened up its centralized structure, got rid of layers of middle management, and put the onus on product development teams to come up with new ideas. The vision from top management was to change Motorola's image by launching superior, edgy products. As some teams at Motorola found out, however, a looser and more decentralized organizational structure posed a significant challenge. Indeed, the strategy didn't produce much—that is, until the Razr team emerged.[5]

Razr was a team on a mission: it would develop a cooler and sleeker phone than anything the world had seen. Cool and sleek was nothing new, but this team planned to produce a phone that would surpass anything that had come before, a veritable "razor" of a phone. Adding to the technical challenge, the team faced a competitive climate in which so-called smartphones—offering a multitude of functions such as e-mail and Internet browsing—were all the rage.

The challenge of bucking industry trends, however, was matched with what the team was up against at Motorola itself. As other teams had discovered, Razr found that despite the company's strategy of depending on entrepreneurship in its product development teams, no road map existed for how to actually pull off such a feat. The Razr team's great ideas, vision, and engineering brilliance was not enough. Somehow the team had to find a way to get the resources it needed to push through a big, unorthodox, and expensive project in a large, orthodox, and cash-strapped organization (though Motorola had begun loosening up its organizational structure, that didn't necessarily mean its culture wasn't as conservative and risk averse as ever). The answer? The Razr team looked outward, by lobbying R&D managers, marketing executives, and the CEO himself and by relentlessly communicating its vision of how the team's ideas linked to the troubled firm's new vision.

We will return in future chapters to exactly how the Razr team accomplished this feat. But for now, it is enough to point out that radical changes and a loosening up in organizational structures at companies like Motorola have created relationships that are less about command-and-control from the executive level and more about entrepreneurship at the operational level. This entrepreneurship is about coming up with new ideas to satisfy customer needs. It is also about making vertical linkages to match new ideas with the firm's overall strategic direction and even about helping reshape that strategy based on what is going on at the operational level. As a result, a lot of the leadership responsibilities in an organization rests with teams that cross hierarchical and functional lines.

In effect, the new order requires leadership that connects all levels of the firm. In addition to loosening up organizational structures, firms have to align the voice and vision of teams like Razr with corporate goals, like shifting the stodgy image of Motorola. Organizations that can create these matches across objectives above and below will be the winners in this competitive race. And it is X-teams that move across boundaries and bring all the players together to discover these matches and to keep innovation moving along.

But why has this decentralization of the old organizational structures come about in the first place? As we've mentioned, competition has become fiercer in general. But what's more, the *nature* of competition has changed dramatically. It is about being fast, about being adaptive, and above all, about being innovative—something that is virtually impossible for a traditional command-and-control organization to pull off.

### From Tight to Loose

Having emerged from a long period of cost cutting in the wake of the dot-com bust, many firms have again started to focus on top-line growth—through either mergers and acquisitions or internal growth. The first has proved extremely difficult to achieve. A string of high-profile cases—including, for example, the arduous merger between transportation giants Daimler-Benz and Chrysler to form DaimlerChrysler—have left many boards hesitant about this route. Instead, firms are increasingly turning to internal growth, a strategy that relies on innovation—that is, new ideas to develop new markets and new product offerings.

Consider GE, the 130-year-old flagship of American industry, whose CEO (Jeffrey Immelt) is attempting a radical reinvention, staking GE's future growth on "breath-taking, mind-blowing, world-rattling technological innovation."[6] Early during his tenure, soon after succeeding the legendary Jack Welch as CEO, Immelt told a group of top managers that the company was going to "put growth on steroids," that the growth was going to be organic, and that it was going to be based on innovation. He then ordered them to come up with big ideas for new businesses, or "imagination breakthroughs."

The new innovation-based competition has changed the demands on organizations dramatically. It's no longer solely up to the executive level to ensure innovation and fast adaptation. The world has become too complex. Today, it's the front lines that have the most information and knowledge about the customer, market, technology, regions, local demands, cultural expectations, and so on. Leadership, therefore, must be pushed from the executive level to the operational level, with rapidly flowing dialogue between them. All of this adds up to a move from a tight structure of command-and-control toward a looser organization of coordinate-and-cultivate. In other words, the executive level needs to create an organization that cultivates entrepreneurial activity, but it also needs to keep some control by coordinating that work and supporting those things that align around a vision and strategy. The effects are far reaching and dramatic. At GE, for instance, it has meant a radical transformation of the view of the firm as a collection of multi-billion-dollar businesses to a network of garage-style start-ups.

What does this mean for teams? We've mentioned the need to push leadership to the operational level and the importance of fostering dialogue between the operational and executive levels. This is where teams need to step up to the plate. As we saw in the Razr team example at Motorola, teams can and must take greater control of their own destiny as well as their organization's. For example, more and more, companies are operating based on a global vision from the executive level that then gets adapted and put into action at the operational level.[7] With no clear implementation guidelines coming from above, it is up to the team to link its activities to the strategic direction set at upper levels. This is a challenge, but it is also an opportunity for entrepreneurship. For team members who are innovative and determined, it means they can follow their own minds about how to implement the espoused vision and even possibly change that vision. To pull this off, they have to be able to sell their ideas and get buy-in from top management and other parts of the organization. So they must not only tend to the internal team process but also go outside the team itself.

Consider another case in point: a team caught in the midst of the changing pharmaceutical industry of the late 1990s.

### Team Fox at Pharmaco

As one of the world's largest pharmaceutical firms, Pharmaco is a true poster child for the recent sea change in the drug industry.[8] It was operating in an environment where new technologies for developing innovative drugs have shown such breathtaking potential that they seemed the stuff of science fiction novels. The deciphering of the human genome is unraveling the mysteries of human life. Scientists have radically increased our understanding of disease. New technology is turning drug discovery from a random mixing of chemicals in a tube to an automated large-scale process. But even with all of that promise, research productivity in the "Big Pharma" firms has fallen in recent years. As Jerry Karabelas, a former head of pharmaceuticals at Novartis, put it: "Data, data everywhere, and not a drug."[9] The industry has gone through a frenzy of mergers or acquisitions to give productivity a boost, but the disappointing results have continued and true innovation remains elusive.

Meanwhile, most of the innovation in pharmaceuticals has recently come from small new firms. As a result, Big Pharma companies have increasingly shifted their R&D efforts to identifying, evaluating, and buying promising molecules from smaller innovative firms. The story of Team Fox occurred just as this shift started to take place.

In the late 1990s, in accordance with industry trends, Pharmaco had started to loosen up its organizational structure. It had also gone through two mergers in a row. As a result, administrative systems were not fully in place, and the executive level was more involved with structural and legal issues—and with jockeying for position in the emerging power structure—than with the core business of drug development. One new strategic cornerstone was in place, though: in the absence of internal innovative breakthroughs, Pharmaco was going to look outside for new innovations—and it would rely on teams like Fox to find them.

For Team Fox and the firm's other drug development teams, the new strategy combined with a loosening organizational structure meant a lot of room to do things their own way. But it also implied an awesome responsibility to keep creating value. This was reflected in the team name, inspired by Archilochus's poem about the hedgehog and the fox. The hedgehog, the story goes, needs to know only one thing, while the fox needs to know many things. As one member explained, "This team needed to do it all." A particular challenge for Team Fox was that Pharmaco had patented no drugs of the particular kind that they had been asked to buy and develop: anti-inflammatory drugs. The only firms with access to this particular class of drugs were a small group of biotechnology firms.

Had this been a few years back, the team would have enjoyed an explicit and exclusive mandate from the executive level to complete its task. The process would have been rigid and tightly controlled through bureaucratic procedures from the executive level, but the team would also have been assured of management support and consistent attention. This time around Team Fox faced some new challenges. To meet them, Fox's members would have to operate differently from how they had worked in the past—differently from the internally focused teams that had dominated Pharmaco until now.

First, with the executive level taking a hands-off approach, Team Fox would have to build its own case for pouring resources into an expensive and risky project and then pitch it to management in competition with other projects. That's quite different from starting out with the resources and mandate already secured. Second, with many projects competing for a limited pool of researchers to staff their teams with, Team Fox's leaders would have to convince line managers to assign scarce talent to their team. All of these were big challenges, and in the following chapters we will return to Team Fox, the additional challenges it faced, and how it overcame them. But the point we want to make here is that for Team Fox to accomplish its mission meant working and communicating intensely across boundaries, and with the executive level in particular, in ways teams at Pharmaco had not done in the past. From a leadership perspective, Team Fox was actually taking the lead in defining a new way of working, and top management was in follow mode. This role reversal is an essential part of distributed leadership.

The stories of Team Fox, as well as Motorola's Razr team, are not isolated incidents. Consider the garage-style start-ups at GE spawned by Immelt's "imagination breakthrough" strategy. In fact, they are all teams, and it is up to them to get their ventures off the ground and out of the garage—which means somehow distinguishing themselves by explaining how they link up to the overall strategy of the firm.

Or consider the teams that develop new cars for DaimlerChrysler in Detroit. In the wake of a turbulent merger, it's the teams themselves that are responsible for developing the innovative new car models that the company has staked its future on. That's a refreshing challenge for entrepreneurial teams, but it comes with tough goals. The new models must be better, nicer looking, *and* more cost effective than current models. And it is largely up to the team to convince top management that they are.

While each team we've mentioned so far in this chapter is distinct in what it does, the brave new worlds facing all these teams are in fact remarkably similar in important ways. Loosening organizational structures driven by innovation-based competition means that teams have gained more autonomy to do their work. But with increased autonomy comes increased responsibility. They have to work much harder to convince the executive level that what they are doing is worth doing and that it links up with the organization's overall strategy, or that it represents a new strategic direction toward success. This task, in turn, has become even more challenging because of changes in the structure of knowledge.

## Islands of Knowledge

Let's look again at Motorola's Razr team, which early on found itself facing a major predicament. While the idea of producing a cool and sleek phone was simple enough, it turned out that the technical implementation of that vision was not. One particularly thorny problem was related to the antenna needed to send and receive the radio signal. To stay true to the vision of the phone, the antenna had to be integrated in the phone's casing—as opposed to placed on top, which was the standard at the time. The challenge for Razr was to track down the expertise needed to go from sketch to reality. Whereas previous Motorola teams had all the expertise they needed at their fingertips, the world had changed: technologies were evolving at breakneck speed, and increasingly picky customers were demanding more sophisticated products that integrated the best of design and technology. To find the most attractive solution, therefore, Razr team members had to seek sophisticated expertise outside the team itself and even outside the company.

Increasingly fierce and innovation-based competition means that to survive, firms today must command leading-edge information. The challenge is compounded by recent changes in the nature of knowledge. While organizational structures in businesses have only in the past decades begun to transform from pyramid-like hierarchies to looser and flatter structures, the knowledge structures on which those same businesses depend have, by their very natures, always been flat—a collection of islands rather than a mountain.[10] But important changes have emerged in knowledge structures too. In no small part driven by the very same competitive dynamics that have led to changes in organizational structures, the collection of islands is expanding and transforming rapidly—it now consists of many more islands of many more different kinds. In fact, to a great extent, these changes have had a role in accelerating the need for the adaptive, loose structures that we just described.

First, scientific and technical knowledge critical for success in innovation-driven environments is becoming much more complex and advanced, on the one hand, and much more dispersed, on the other. The fact that these forces are at work simultaneously makes the task to keep up so much harder. A second major change in knowledge structures is the need to keep track of rapidly changing markets, and a third challenge stems from the need for real-time knowledge about fast-moving competitors. All three challenges are intensified by the fact that the sheer volume of all kinds of knowledge is continuously and exponentially increasing.[11]

Consider the first change. The dependence on increasingly advanced—and fast-advancing—scientific and technical knowledge has driven value-creating activity in organizations to become ever-more specialized. This is reflected in a growing number of people with doctoral degrees not only in engineering-heavy industries, such as biotechnology and computing, but also in service industries, such as banking and insurance. To stay on top of their respective fields, these experts need to spend a lot of time staying abreast of knowledge in their specialties and socializing with their peers. Hence, a formal hierarchical position says less and less about the type and quality of knowledge residing there.

As knowledge specialization has increased, so has the dispersion of knowledge—both in the organizational and the geographic sense. This is partly a direct effect of specialization. As knowledge becomes more advanced, there is only so much room for breadth in the knowledge repository of one organization or one organizational unit. It is also an effect of changes in industry structure. For example, in the wake of the molecular biology revolution, knowledge seen as key in modern drug development was suddenly found outside the established pharmaceutical firms, in small biotech start-ups scattered around university campuses in Silicon Valley and Boston.

That brings us to the second major change in knowledge structures—and the mirror image of more complex yet more dispersed technical knowledge: a fast-moving marketplace with sophisticated and differentiated customers whose requirements can change in the blink of an eye. Similarly, in the wings waits the third major change: more competitors than ever before, eager to take advantage of disruptive change and outmaneuver slow incumbents. In addition to their larger numbers, these competitors are smarter and more aggressive, and they come in more forms and from more places than in the past. Keeping track of these players is not easy, but competitive success increasingly depends on it.

What does this mean for teams? In their role as leaders of innovation, they must find the knowledge they need outside their immediate environment, and often outside the organization, and bring it in. Great specialization, combined with the increased rate of knowledge dissemination across many places, means that teams often won't have the knowledge needed to complete the task at hand. The knowledge may be technical—such as input from the latest science in a particular discipline—but it could also be information related to what customers demand and what competitors are doing. Lack of such real-time information about fast-changing technologies, customers, and competitors can spell disaster for a product development team—such as developing a technically sophisticated product that customers no longer want for a market segment that competitors have already filled. In other words, unless a team pays close and continuous attention to the changing external environment, the product it develops may have turned obsolete even before launch.

But there's still more reason for teams to tap outside sources for knowledge: the time pressure to stay abreast with the competition means that teams cannot afford to reinvent the wheel. Odds are that other teams within the organization or in other firms have found solutions to the very problems the team is facing. Teams need to find these other teams, learn from them, and borrow best practices.

Consider again our example of Pharmaco and Team Fox's task to develop a new anti-inflammatory drug. Over the years Pharmaco had accumulated impressive capabilities in drug development—but not in the area of anti-inflammation. Hence, Team Fox had to look outside for a promising molecule. In addition, while Fox had access to best-in-class clinical capabilities, it lacked leading-edge technical expertise pertaining to the early stages of development. But Team Fox faced more challenges still. Since it had not worked with this kind of drug before, Team Fox lacked the often tacit knowledge of how to set up and carry out the complex procedures involved in researching such molecules. To succeed, Fox needed to figure out where to find this expertise and how to bring it in. The task was further complicated because Team Fox was hoping to make a splash in a sophisticated and dynamic marketplace. Accurate information on the whereabouts of customers and competitors would be critical. In the highly secretive world of pharmaceuticals, this data would also be very challenging for team members to get their hands on.

Similarly, GE's "garage" teams have often found themselves lacking internal knowledge to meet CEO Immelt's challenging "imagination breakthroughs" strategy. For example, one team started to work on a supercompact jet engine but found that, while GE had world-class jet engine capabilities, it lacked leading-edge knowledge of how to make such engines compact. Another team, in GE's home-security division, was convinced that alarm systems could be dramatically improved but lacked the software skills required to make its vision a reality. To find what they needed, these teams had to venture far beyond their own domain.

The teams of DaimlerChrysler charged with developing new, cost-effective car models provide yet another example. Although opportunities for cost cutting could be found in the early stages of the design process, the design engineers lacked the knowledge needed about the purchasing process to realize this potential. That knowledge resided elsewhere.

The problem that all of these teams have in common is that, while competitive demands have become tougher, the critical knowledge needed to beat the competition has become ever-more complex, fast advancing, and spread out. The knowledge teams need to accomplish their tasks increasingly can't be found within the team or even the company itself. Instead, these teams have found it critical to span their boundaries in pursuit of the knowledge they need. Those changes in knowledge structures also have far-reaching implications for the structure of the very tasks in which teams are engaged.

## Expanding Task Boundaries

Let's return to Team Fox at Pharmaco, which faced a challenging job indeed. First, team members had to work overtime just to identify a potential blockbuster drug outside Pharmaco and the expertise needed to evaluate and develop it. Second, they also had to constantly stay in touch with the executive level to make sure they would have the resources and buy-in to keep the project on track. But they had to keep a third ball in the air as well: throughout the process they needed to coordinate and synchronize their work with other teams. These teams worked on other drugs, but they were part of the same family of products and used the same resources. That meant Team Fox often needed to collaborate with them. For example, this almost always meant coordinating Fox's task with a great number of other teams when planning the design of labs, when purchasing active ingredients, and so on. In addition, Team Fox needed to coordinate the marketing message with other drugs in the pipeline. A unifying message to the potential customer was important to build a brand in anti-inflammatory drugs.

All of this is to illustrate, of course, the changes in task structures inherent in today's organization—and what that means for teams. While organizational life was never characterized by perfect order and stability, in many old-style centralized organizations, goals were typically known, the environment was relatively stable, and tasks tended to be repetitive, relatively unchanged, and carefully partitioned. But the same competitive pressures that have driven changes in organizational structures and knowledge structures have also had a profound impact on the structure of tasks. In the wake of loosening organizations and changing knowledge structures, teams depend on changing knowledge bases and processes that span people and units horizontally, which effectively cuts across hierarchies, units, and teams. Changes in the organizational structures and knowledge structures are thus expanding the boundaries of the teams' tasks themselves, changing the scope of the work that they do. For example, if a team does not have the knowledge that it needs to complete a task, it may have to create a lateral link to another team that does. Its task may then have to be coordinated with the work of the other team, schedules may have to be synchronized, and so on. Such interdependencies increase the complexity and difficulty of a task considerably.

Perhaps the most important driver of changing task structures, however, is strategic and dictated by fiercer and fiercer competition. Bundling has become a buzzword in strategies about selling products and ideas in a marketplace that is relentlessly putting pressure on the prices firms can charge—the idea is that firms can add to their profit margins by offering bundles of products to their customers. Perhaps the most well-known, and certainly very successful, example is Microsoft's Windows platform strategy, which encourages customers to buy a whole family of software products that are compatible with the operating system. Pharmaco's strategy of marketing a family of anti-inflammatory drugs offers another case in point. Bundled products require simultaneous and coordinated work from multiple parts of the organization. Furthermore, selling system solutions requires input from many more areas than selling components or stand-alone products does, which creates interdependence.

In addition, by pooling resources and sharing product platforms, dramatic cost savings are pursued. At DaimlerChrysler, for example, the quest for realizing efficiencies in purchasing means linking the company's various processes for designing new cars to each other, as well as to key suppliers.

The increased need for speed has triggered a move from sequences of subtasks to reciprocal interdependence. No longer do design engineers simply design a car model and throw it over the wall to manufacturing—risking delays from unexpected problems when the car is actually being made. Instead, design engineers talk to manufacturing engineers about what they're thinking and to see whether new ideas can be implemented effectively. The approach is interdependent and iterative, not sequential.

The need for speed also creates task decomposition. A task may be broken down into multiple pieces to be completed by different work units. This increases the demand for coordination across units to make sure that the pieces come together again effectively.

At the center of this process, we find teams that need to coordinate with each other to make sure that what they do fits the product family, the system solution, or the manufacturing platform seamlessly. To make things even more complicated, in an ever-changing competitive landscape, this has to be done fast. New strategic imperatives of speed and synergies for firms, then, have created greater interdependence and more work for teams.

Consider again the Razr team. The unique product design it chose came with a tricky coordination task. The marketing people, production managers, and accountants whom Razr depended on were used to working with very different parameters. Making the interactions work seamlessly was not an easy feat. Similarly, the teams at Microsoft, DaimlerChrysler, and Pharmaco all found their tasks interconnected with the work of others outside the team. Witness the complex mosaic of tests that is involved in drug development. For Team Fox this meant orchestrating complex and highly knowledge-intensive subtasks across a vast array of disciplines and phases of development.

It's important to note that for all of these teams, great internal teamwork was not enough to complete their tasks. They needed to coordinate their tasks with other teams with which they were interdependent as well. This, it turns out, is a vastly complicated task in itself—one that we will examine in depth in the next chapter.

## The Need for Distributed Leadership

We have mentioned several times how in the wake of monumental changes in the organizational landscape, distributed leadership has emerged as fundamentally important. In an increasingly competitive, complex, and fast-paced world in which information and expertise are distributed across multiple individuals and firms, distributed leadership throughout the organization is crucial.[12] Effective leadership at the top is simply not enough. Instead, leadership needs to be present at all levels of the firm.

While the CEO may develop strategies, he or she must count on the input of others who may have more knowledge about the sales trends or the competition. Also, the CEO must rely on others to adapt those strategies to meet local conditions and culture, as well as to take the lead on the front lines, managing customers, suppliers, and sudden crises. Then leaders at all levels need to work together to make sure that their own actions mesh with those of others throughout the organization.

Distributed leadership, then, is part of the new organization—and it is teams that enable this leadership form. It is teams that are now called on to put breadth and detail into visions and strategies from on high as they become the eyes of the organization, produce the products, enact the processes, and spread new practices that become the real output of the organization. Teams are now called on to translate big ideas into concrete projects and action, which, in turn, shape future strategies and new potential visions of the firm.

Unquestionably, the many changes in organizational life driven by innovation-driven competition and other environmental shifts have created a whole new world for teams—one in which they play a more critical role than ever before. Not only must teams work within new structures that have become loose, spread-out systems with numerous alliances rather than multilevel centralized organizations. Not only are the knowledge structures within which teams must work—the very ways they get information to complete their tasks—increasingly complex, externally dispersed, and rapidly changing. Not only are the tasks teams must do increasingly interwoven with other teams' tasks throughout the organization and even outside it. In the wake of these challenges, and the imperative of distributed leadership this new organizational landscape has created, it has fallen to the teams at the front lines to exert effective leadership at all levels.

In this chapter we have stressed the importance of new competitive pressures and how this has led to changes in organizational structure, information, and task interdependence. But there are other pressures on the horizon that will add to the complexity of the work in teams and organizations. In particular, global warming, poverty, pollution, and political instability appear to be getting worse. There is the increasing sense both within society and organizations themselves that government and nongovernmental organizations will not be able to deal with these issues single-handedly. Instead organizations will need to get involved in cross-sector work to help solve these difficult problems that require innovative solutions. Here again, much of this work will be given to teams who will have to reach beyond their boundaries to work cooperatively with others within and outside their organizations to meet these consequential challenges of our time.

All of this requires external outreach. Even the smoothest internal team process matters little unless the team connects with stakeholders and resources outside itself. Internal process alone will not transform a team into a vehicle for innovation and change. Internal process alone will not help a team take on the distributed leadership challenge. Trouble is, the challenges related to working externally have not been matched with a set of tools that help teams address those issues and avoid the vicious spiral we illustrated in the last chapter. The good news is that such tools do exist. Let us begin by examining the first of the three principles by which X-teams guide themselves and that we began to describe in the introduction of this book: the external activities that a team can foster to meet the new challenges.

# PART II

# What Works

# THREE

# X-Team Principle 1

## *External Activity*

A S PART OF A MAJOR REORGANIZATION at BellCo, a telecommunications company that sells equipment to businesses, the Big Bank team was formed.[1] From now on the firm would not be selling specific products to a general market, but sophisticated systems that bundled together several products and had specialized features for specific customer needs. As part of this change, the sales force was being reconfigured into teams to serve particular industry segments—like banking, software, and pharmaceuticals—rather than geographic areas. For the company this was a major reorganization designed to sell higher-margin products through industry specialization, thus improving profitability and hopefully increasing market share.

The Big Bank team consisted of five members: two salespeople (Jean-Yves and Vicki, who was the formal team leader), two implementers (Randy and Russell), and one systems designer (Robert). They were initially not sure what their approach to selling to the banking segment would be but decided they had to figure it out. While sitting around a large table at a local bar after the new organization was announced, Vicki put a stop to the conversation about "waiting for the new guidelines." She advocated that waiting was a complete waste of time and said that the directives from central were not going to clarify things anyway.

Vicki was right, of course. While top management had a great new strategy, the implementation effort would have to fall to the teams themselves. Corporate directives could only cover so much ground; each new team would have to invent its own way of meeting the challenges posed by this new approach. Leadership shifted from the executive suite to the teams that would breathe life into top management's ideas. But Vicki's determined attitude opened up a whole new set of questions that the team would need to deal with if it hoped to take on this leadership role. How, for example, would the team go about getting all the information it needed? And once it uncovered that knowledge, how would members get senior management on board with the pitch they wanted to make to customers? Finally, the fact that the Big Bank team members needed to sell communications systems to banking businesses would involve a complicated set of steps. Not only would they need to match their product with customer needs; they also would have to get their bids accepted and come up with an installation strategy and process. These were just the basic tasks that Big Bank faced. Now Vicki and her team needed to find a way to accomplish them.

Up to this point we've looked at examples of teams—like the Northwest consulting team, Team Fox in the pharmaceutical company, and Motorola's Razr team—facing the same kinds of dilemmas the Big Bank team was confronting, and we've watched them begin to resolve those dilemmas. But what specific tools did those teams need to foster to accomplish what they did? How would a team like Big Bank begin to address the issues it faced while avoiding the vicious downward spiral we described in chapter 1?

A good place to start is by engaging in rigorous, continuous external activity in addition to managing internal team dynamics. High-performing teams manage across their boundaries, reaching out to find the information they need, understand the context in which they work, manage the politics and power struggles that surround any team initiative, get support for their ideas, and coordinate with the myriad other groups that are key to a team's success. This is the first of our three X-team principles: *X-teams engage in high levels of external activity.*

But what does effective external activity consist of exactly? We've found that it falls into three distinct subactivities: scouting, ambassadorship, and task coordination.

While teams often think they understand what the task is, what the customer wants, where the technology is moving, and what the marketplace and culture expect, they often miss the mark. What many teams do not fully grasp or appreciate is that, even if their members are all stars with the best ideas, team members must get the information that's critical to carrying out their task. Without it, the fact that those members are stars matters little. Teams, therefore, need to work hard to understand others' expectations and continue to update their information about key stakeholders. They need to know where critical information and expertise reside, both inside and outside the organization. They need to take stock of how the world has changed and what new threats and opportunities have emerged. They need to have a good model of what the outside world is like so they can shift and adapt accordingly. In short, teams need to engage in "scouting" activity.

Even so, if the team members cannot make their case to top management, cannot connect their work to the firm's strategy, and cannot garner resources and cooperation from others, then all the work of creating the breakthrough product or the hottest idea may be for naught. Thus, it is often up to team members to lobby for resources, get early buy-in for their ideas, and keep working for support from top managers. All of this is what we call "ambassadorship."

Finally, many a team has failed not because members neglected to do everything they set out to do but because another group did not provide the appropriate input; because members could not negotiate the right deal with another group, inside or outside the company; or simply because another group found that it did not really want what the team had produced. While many failed teams blame these other groups for their problems, finger pointing does not usually help. Apart from not helping the outcome one iota, casting blame also creates a lot of unwanted negative feelings all around, and team members in the end may take the heat for that negativity anyway. Here again team members can take a more proactive role in managing the interdependencies with other parts of the firm, and groups outside the firm, by engaging in "task coordination."

As we already have noted, however, it is not always intuitive or natural for team members to engage in all of these aspects of external activity, especially early on. Such activities are hard to do. Just when the team members come together and anxiety is highest, just when the team wants to find solutions to its tough problems and move into action—members must come face-to-face with a grim reality. They must admit to themselves that they may not fully understand their task or the context in which they are operating. They must confront a world in which their expectations of what must be done and those of key stakeholders may differ. On top of these concerns is the pressure to come up with new ideas quickly and get other groups to cooperate and convince top management to buy into these ideas—even when the ideas are not fully developed.

All of this is to say that teams have to accept that, to really succeed, they will not have free reign but rather must link to top management initiatives—not always knowing what these are from the outset. And they can't do this alone. They are dependent on a whole host of other individuals and groups that may not have incentive to help. And so rather than reducing their anxiety, or enabling instant problem solving, team members must actively deal with their own anxiety—and then go about trying to get the information they need to move ahead.

That's where the team leader's job comes in. Leaders need to create a safe environment to deal with members' understandable—but potentially debilitating—free-flowing anxiety and provide a structure that will integrate internal with external activity. They also must have a clear idea of what needs to take place to engage effectively in scouting, ambassadorship, and task coordination. Luckily, leadership functions for X-teams are spread across many individuals, so these tasks do not remain the sole responsibility of one person. Thus, X-teams themselves are a form of distributed leadership. Let's look more closely at what the first of these tools, scouting, does to help teams break out of their often myopic internal focus.

## Scouting

Let's return to our opening example of the Big Bank team. When Vicki, the official team leader, halted the conversation about waiting for more direction from the top, she had an alternate plan in mind. Wouldn't it be quicker, more informative, and more empowering, she suggested, if the team members spread out and asked other groups in the company how they expected to work with the Big Bank team in the new design?

And so scouting began with small, careful steps. Members split into different pairs and went to talk to people in technical support, installation, and sales. They asked lots and lots of questions: When we have a potential sale and we need help, whom should we contact? What are you going to need to know? How can we best prepare to work with you on these kinds of accounts? Sometimes the people they spoke to had the answers, sometimes team members got sent to someone else, and sometimes no one knew and they started to make up some procedures that they thought might work. And then they all met and pooled the information they had gathered. With a clear task of scouting and data flowing in about what their new world looked like, the Big Bank members began to feel less anxious and more confident. They began to create a mental map of how things might work and set out to learn more.

Just as the task of a scouting party in the wilderness is to carefully explore and gather information about the surrounding terrain to see whether it is safe to move ahead, so is the role of scouting activity for an X-team like Big Bank. Scouting is aimed at understanding what's out there so that team members know whether they can proceed or whether they need to make adjustments to what they are currently doing. Scouting allows the team to predict the rough spots ahead and to get a sense of how dangerous the terrain really is.

As the Big Bank team came to understand, scouting includes learning about the expectations of other key constituencies and gathering relevant information throughout the company and the industry. It involves extensive searching to understand who has knowledge and expertise and what current trends in the marketplace are. It means investigating customers, new technologies, and the competition. It may even mean discovering that the firms you thought were the competition are not your biggest threat—that a set of low-cost producers in China, rather than that behemoth down the street, is stealing your market share. In short, scouting means being open to new trends and updating your view of the world. Scouting enables team members to make sense of the world around them and to come up with a common map of that external terrain.[2]

Scouting also means finding key centers of expertise and information. Teams we have met and worked with use many different modes of scouting, from the ambitious and expensive (e.g., hiring consultants) to the quick and cheap (e.g., spending an hour on the Internet or having a cup of coffee with an old college professor). While a lot of scouting is done through observation and conversation, team members also have used surveys, interviews, archival data, and consultant and analyst reports to learn more about what different groups are thinking and doing.

Beyond specific techniques, scouting requires a mind-set and culture of awareness. While Andrew Grove's advice to "be paranoid" may seem a bit strong, it speaks to the need to be on the alert for big shifts (what Grove calls "strategic inflection points") in customer demand, market focus, technological breakthroughs, and strategic direction that have implications for the team.[3] If a team is working on a product while customer demand is swinging in a totally different direction, then team members need to be aware of this trend so that they can determine their response.

Additionally, effective teams monitor how much information they need. As problems become more complex and information more dispersed, the task of scouting becomes more difficult and intense. Add to that the fast rate of change in technology and markets, and scouting often needs to be ongoing, rather than a one-time exercise. Sometimes scouting continues throughout a team's lifetime because each phase of work demands scouting in new directions and changes in the environment may render the team's work obsolete. But for other teams, extensive scouting early on to get the lay of the land is all that's needed. For these teams, too much scouting can lead to analysis paralysis and impede the movement from exploring an idea to actually implementing a project.

In short, scouting is a multifaceted activity that involves three main tasks: staking out the organizational terrain; monitoring external trends and the activities of customers and competitors; and vicarious learning.

### Investigating the Organizational Terrain

Getting a sense of what a team's task actually is, who the key players are, and what everyone's expectations for the final product are is scouting's key task. Scouting also involves uncovering the often tacit, unwritten cultural expectations that others have for the team. While team members may think they know the answers to these questions, their answers may be outdated, biased, or simply wrong. Starting with a fresh outlook, then, and spending the time to figure out how other firm members view their work is critical.

For Big Bank that meant doing some of the initial scouting activity already described and then getting in touch with corporate to ask these questions: How would the new compensation system work? What would team members have to sell in what quantities to make those bonuses? Members got in touch with the designers of the new organization and asked exactly how they imagined the teams would work, asking questions like: What were teams expected to do in what period of time? Did they just have to identify key prospects in the new marketplace, or were sales expected in the first quarter? In short, these team members tried to figure out as much as they could about the new terrain they were facing.

Part of what Big Bank members came to understand was that the corporate design group had created not just a new organizational design to improve the company's competitive position but also a design that required cultural changes. Whereas customers who needed products used to come to the team, now the team would have to be much more aggressive in searching out customers and tailoring solutions to their needs. But this had never been done before at BellCo, and it was clear that the guidelines from corporate did not explain how team members would gain the expertise and cooperation they needed from others or how they would learn how to sell. While other teams waited for instructions and continued to work in the old way, the Big Bank team decided to meet this new challenge head-on.

### Investigating Customers, Competitors, and Current Trends

While some scouting takes place within the organization, a large part revolves around understanding what goes on outside the organization. Learning about customer needs is often a high priority, but this form of scouting may also need to take place with suppliers, competitors, the technical and scientific communities, consultants, industry experts, and so on. The key is to figure out the critical groups that team members need to understand and then go out and learn what those people are thinking, feeling, considering, expecting, admiring, fearing, and wanting. For some teams the key is the most experimental customer, for others it is finding the latest technologies or that critical piece of information, and for some it is simply about being one step ahead of competitors. Whatever the needs, a new understanding and mapping of these domains is crucial.

The Big Bank team knew it now had to focus on selling systems to large banks. The focus of external scouting became the customer and the competition. They were the new kids on the block, and they felt the pressure to move quickly up the learning curve. So team leader Vicki and her cosalesperson, Jean-Yves, started to read lots of literature from the banking industry. They were looking for new trends and needs. Since they were the ones who would have to do most of the selling, they had to know how to talk to their customers in new ways and with more knowledge than they currently had. They visited some of their existing clients, the ones with whom they had great relationships, and told those clients about the changes at BellCo. They started to ask about whether there was a need for such systems and about clients' required features and price ranges. They asked, "If we gave you something like this, would you be interested?" and "If not, why not?"

While this was going on, team members Randy, Russell, and Robert were busy trying to learn about what kinds of systems their competitors were installing. Since they were the ones who had the technical training and the ones who would have to design and implement the system, they were very interested in the types of systems their competitors were selling and what it took to move from initial sale to final approval. They went to a bank that had switched to another vendor to get a more complex system and asked why the customer had made the change. They studied the system and compared it to what they could produce. Then they got on the Web and looked at the offerings from all their competitors. This was the beginning of a comparison chart that the team would later use to show what the company could do that the competition could not. While Randy, Russell, and Robert were at it, they tried to figure out the sign-off process for such a system at the customer site. Who would have to approve such a purchase, and what constraints was that person under?

Consider again Team Fox in the pharmaceutical firm introduced earlier. While the Big Bank team's scouting activity focused on the customer and the competition, Fox's members had to search for scientific knowledge outside its borders. Their challenge was to find the type of molecule needed for a new drug that was not available inside the organization itself. Hence, the first order of business for team members was to scan the globe for leads. This involved attending conferences, mining databases, and tracking down old friends in the industry as well as in academia for advice. In the end, the molecule that became the raison d'être of the project was found via a tip-off from a subsidiary an ocean away.

### Vicarious Learning

Scouting also involves what we call "vicarious team learning," in which teams learn how to do a task by observing others outside the team or talking to them about their experiences.[4] In this case scouting is not about understanding the expectations of others within the firm nor about incorporating information from customers, competitors, or suppliers. Rather, here team members can learn ways to do their task by copying or modifying what other teams have done.

In our work, vicarious learning was pivotal in enabling teams to do better than teams that had done the task before. Vicarious learning takes many forms but usually concentrates on scouting around for teams that have done a similar task. Then all kinds of information can be gleaned, such as: What mistakes did you make (so that we don't have to repeat them)? What is the scope of this project? Which team was most successful before, and what did its members do? Who gave you the best information, and whom do we need to talk to about this? How did you do this part of the task, or can we use your data?

Team members can save lots of time by borrowing machinery, copying documents and contracts, and then adapting them to the needs of their task, learning which consultants were helpful and which ones were just a waste of time. Team members also can ascertain from others how to provide the most value to the firm (what's really important here?). Teams can build very effectively on the work of earlier projects, creating a stream of learning across projects in the firm. Over time, we've seen this kind of vicarious learning help teams become more and more successful.

For the Big Bank team, vicarious learning was a problem since the team was one of the first in the company to try to sell under the new system. Interestingly, one of the team members, Jean-Yves, had a friend in another industry who had already made a successful transition from component to systems selling. Jean-Yves went to visit his friend, notebook in hand, and took as many notes as possible about the steps needed to make this transition. He came back with a number of ideas that helped the Big Bank team move into systems selling at an even faster rate than other teams.

Vicarious learning from other organizations and, in fact, from other industries is a core practice in a number of organizations. When a team from BP wanted to learn more about standardization, the teammates didn't look at oil and gas companies but at car companies that had already developed the idea of common platforms across different car models. When a team in the financial services industry wanted to learn about improving customer satisfaction, members did not look at other companies in the industry but at Neiman Marcus, a leading department store known for treating customers well. When the product design firm IDEO wanted to redesign operating rooms, it spent a day looking at how a NASCAR pit crew worked to learn how teams with emergencies, time constraints, numerous experts, and safety concerns worked together. This kind of vicarious learning can help teams take quantum leaps in innovation since ideas that are totally new to the industry can be more quickly adopted into practice.

But innovation can also come from intensive vicarious learning within the firm. Recall the Razr team, introduced in the last chapter, which needed to figure out how to make a sleek phone that would stomp the competition and revive Motorola's stodgy image. Such a complex design required complicated technological footwork. Razr team members started by looking at what other teams had done before them. They looked not only at what had worked and what had not worked but also at what had been discarded. The team "found that the engineers had already cast aside some clever and promising directions based on very informal discussions with various expert groups."[5] The team solved a number of technological challenges, like mounting a camera on a tiny phone and developing a keypad that was etched directly onto the phone, by repackaging existing technologies developed—and sometimes thrown away— by other teams.

By learning vicariously, then, team members can avoid making the same mistakes as others, shortcut the work that they have to do, and start working at a higher level of understanding and competence than teams that don't engage in this type of scouting activity.

### *When Scouting Goes Overboard*

While this section has been full of examples of effective scouting, teams can often get stuck in scouting mode or do a poor job of scouting.[6] In the former case, team members never feel as if they have enough information and they just keep collecting more and more. But at some point deadlines kick in, and the team needs to segue from exploring the terrain to moving ahead. For some teams this transition is impossible to make, and they flounder.[7] These teams get caught in a continuous search, start to let deadlines slip, and are never able to move on. In the case of poor scouting, teams can learn the wrong things from others, or innovation can actually be stifled as teams simply copy old ideas without creating new ones. These teams get caught in the one-mold-fits-all trap and then have a harder time in another facet of external activity: ambassadorship.

## Ambassadorship

Let's return to our example of the Big Bank team. Members there worked hard to combine all the information they were collecting from their scouting activities. They needed to turn that knowledge into a pitch for the customers whom they saw as having the highest potential for buying the systems that they knew they could build and deliver. As they prepared to bid on a big project, they asked the VP of commercial to go along with them to show that the organization's upper levels were committed to the product. In preparing the VP for this meeting, the team was able to showcase all the work it had done and demonstrate an ability to work within the new organizational design. The VP, for his part, was relieved to find that there were teams in his organization that were making the changes that corporate required. He was able to report this progress to his superiors, while simultaneously using the Big Bank team as an example of success within his own organization. Since a number of teams were very busy complaining about how the new system could not work, he now had a response. Luckily, that sale went through, and the VP volunteered to go on other customer visits with the Big Bank team, which was a big advantage for the team.

As this example begins to illustrate, ambassadorship is aimed at managing up the organizational hierarchy. It includes marketing the project and the team to top management, lobbying for resources, maintaining the team's reputation, and keeping track of allies and adversaries. When he was visiting the MIT Sloan School of Management, John McNerney, the former CEO of 3M and current CEO of Boeing, told us the importance of integrating vertically—linking the top level of the firm to the operational level (not to be confused with the "vertical integration" strategy used in many firms). This is the way that an organization can achieve alignment between the strategy and those who must implement the strategy. It is ambassadorship that creates the dialogue up and down the organizational hierarchy and achieves this integration. For example, the members of the Northwest consulting team, introduced in chapter 1, came up with the idea of creating a cutting-edge school evaluation program to help meet customer needs in their region. The team members reported on this work to the president of the organization, and it meshed perfectly with his idea to spread innovative new practices throughout all the regions. The president then asked all the teams to create a similar program. Here knowledge of what works with the customer becomes integrated with organizational strategy. This integration up and down the organization, with different levels relying on and helping each other, is at the heart of distributed leadership.

Ambassadorship, then, helps the team link its work to key strategic initiatives or possibly even change those initiatives in an organization—and it alerts team members to shifting organizational strategies and political upheaval so that potential threats can be identified and damage limited. In short, ambassadorial activity links the team to higher levels in the firm and gets buy-in and support from people with influence. Sometimes linking means that the team moves in the direction set by top management; at other times, however, it means lobbying to change the views at the top. Finally, ambassadorial activity helps a team manage the power and politics that are a part of every organization.

### *Linking to Strategic Initiatives and Getting Early Buy-In*

One of the major problems in organizations today is finding a way to link top management and its strategic initiatives to lower-level people who are interacting with customers, designing and building new products, and carrying out the firm's core work. Ambassadorship is one way that a team can be proactive in connecting its work to new strategic directions. By linking to these new directions, the team often finds it easier to get top management's attention and support.

Not only does such ambassadorship help get buy-in and support from top management; it can also help shape the team's task and goals. For example, a team from BP was given the task of improving one aspect of the project management process for large projects. Team members wanted to work on how to better staff projects with the right people. Because this was too broad a task, members set out to talk to more senior managers to seek sponsorship and get ideas about the best way to focus their activity. In talking to one senior manager, who later became their sponsor, they learned that she was working on a talent management plan for the firm. It turned out that if they focused their work on a particular aspect of the staffing process, then their work could also be of help to her work. So in this way, they found a way to narrow their scope, get senior management support, and provide key information to the firm that could be used on multiple fronts. Everyone was pleased.

In contrast, some teams decide that they know better and go off on their own anyway. That was the case with a software development team we know of, which ended up not getting managerial support and buy-in.[8]

This software team heard that one of its Japanese customers was interested in a new version of its product, Entry, which would work on a recently developed platform. The six engineers in the team who were managing the project (known in the company as the "gods") decided that such a step would be important to the team, so they stopped all work on the current version of the product in order to adapt Entry to the new platform. Team members worked long hours and weekends, but after weeks of hard work, the proposal was rejected and another team was chosen to do the new project. After "forty-nine days in hell" (the team members' term for the time that they had spent working on the new product proposal that was ultimately rejected), the team reverted to its original configuration to do its work. Members viewed the rejection of their proposal as a declaration of war with top management, and relations were strained for many months following the decision. Team members felt as if they had come up with a great proposal for a great product and that management just didn't appreciate or understand their ideas. Shortly after this time the "gods" left the company.

It is important to note that the Entry team members did bring their proposal to top management—but only *after* it was finished. It turns out that the timing of ambassadorial activity is extremely important. Getting buy-in and support early in the process is essential. Early involvement helps mesh new product ideas with top management's directives, allowing for input when it can truly be incorporated into the team's work, not when that work is a fait accompli. Perhaps the most critical element of early involvement is that once the top managers have had a say in the idea, they are more committed to ensuring its success.

And yet the Entry team did not even stop to think about getting buy-in and support. Once its members had got hold of a great idea, they were ready to speed into action. Also, they simply could not imagine that the top management team would not see this opportunity the same way that they saw it. It was so clear to them that this was the way to go that they slipped back into the old internal model. They worked to motivate all the team members and allocate work. They worked to deadlines that would assure that the proposal would be in by the time funding decisions were made. And they simply assumed that all their hard work and great ideas would be recognized and appreciated. Furthermore, they assumed that since they were engineers, it wasn't their job to get buy-in; it was their job to come up with good ideas, and top management's job to recognize quality. Given these assumptions, the lack of funding came as an extra-hard blow and left a sense of betrayal.

### *Lobbying for the Team and Members' Ideas*

Of course, we would not want to leave the impression that ambassadorial activity is just about having teams follow the lead of senior managers. True distributed leadership means that the onus of deciding where to go, what to do, and how to do it shifts across levels and entities. It is this dialogue of integration that the X-team achieves through ambassadorship. Often team members have unique views of customers, markets, new products, better processes, and changes in technologies that come from their scouting activities. They are often the ones who have direct access to shifting trends and to the people who do the firm's primary work. Thus, sometimes the task of ambassadorial activity is to lobby for the team's ideas, to fight for what members think is right, even if top management does not agree. The team members' job then becomes one of converting top managers to their point of view; their job is to give voice to their passion and paint a picture of their visions for the future. Note, however, that even when the task is one of conversion, the conversations start early, and top managers are able to provide input and suggestions on what the final proposal looks like.

For example, the project leader of a new computer design team engaged top management from the very beginning. As the project was being discussed by the operating committee (a top management committee that managed new-product development projects for the firm), the team leader met often with committee members, who wanted the new computer to be a slight change from the existing model. But the leader worked to convince committee members that they should go with a revolutionary design rather than a simple upgrade. Using data that other team members had pulled together in a report on estimated schedules and budgets, he insisted that they had the talent and motivation to make a great product and make it quickly. Furthermore, he thought that the competition was moving faster than any of them expected. It was time for a big move. Finally, the decision was made to go ahead with the project. The leader asked the president of the company and the vice president of R&D to come to the first meeting to explain the importance of the product to the company and to communicate their support for the team. The leader remained in close contact with the president throughout the project—which was ultimately a success.[9]

Of course, not all conversions are successful. Sometimes top management simply does not want to listen to new ideas or thinks that such ideas are not a priority. Here team members can choose to continue their lobbying efforts or move on to something else. There is a fine line between going after what one truly believes in and being labeled a visionary—versus continuing to argue and being labeled as someone who doesn't understand the word *no*. Since the latter is often viewed as career-limiting behavior, it can undermine attempts to change the system in a new direction. This is where being in an X-team takes courage and determination—whether the decision is to fight because members believe in the idea or not to fight because it is not in the best interests of the organization or the team.

Basically, the goals of linking and lobbying are to create this vertical integration between the top of the organization and the operational level. What teams and organizations need to find is a match that satisfies both levels. This is where companies can best leverage the work of the teams and teams can have their ideas heard and implemented. This is exactly what happened in the Razr team when Roger Jellicoe, the formal team leader, brought his idea of a phone that was less than one-half-inch thick to chief marketing officer Geoffrey Frost. Frost was "frustrated with how stodgy [Motorola's] products had become. He wanted a couple of initiatives up and running that would break that image."[10] And suddenly, here was a solution to his problem, coupled with a set of people motivated to make it happen. It was a win-win solution.

### Cultivating Allies and Containing Adversaries

Organizations are political entities. They are arenas in which power gets played out between those who have it and those who want to have it. Here people hoard resources and hold grudges; they guard their turf and strike at those who try to take it away. Even in such a context, however, ambassadorship finds people with power and influence to help protect the team from political machinations and to manage the conflicts that inevitably occur as people try new things that upset the power balance.

For example, the Big Bank team was meeting together one evening in a conference room brainstorming about how they might approach a customer who was leaning toward a competitor. Members considered lowering their price or discounting future products that could be added to the systems. But the particular package that they wanted to offer fell outside the normal guidelines, and they were told that the pricing was unacceptable. This was when the team asked the VP to step in and make an exception. And he did.

A similar kind of protection was offered to the Razr team when Rob Shaddock, the group's general manager, provided "air cover" for the team and the program. Shaddock told others on the executive team, "I don't want anybody to count on something that is this technologically advanced hitting next year. We have to make our companywide plan without it, and if this team delivers on this product, then it is all upside." This kind of freedom made it possible to shortcut many bureaucratic procedures, to operate with what Shaddock called a "stealth approach to the market," and to move quickly through product development by keeping interference minimized. This meant that numerous powerful groups could not have their normal input, a political situation that could not have been contemplated without top management's protection.

### A Cautionary Note on Ambassadorial Behavior

While there is no question that ambassadorial behavior is a key predictor of success for many kinds of teams, there is one important caveat: not all teams that engage in ambassadorial activity are successful.[11] What differentiates high-performing ambassadorial teams from low-performing ones? It turns out that teams that do not do well are those that market and promote their team and the team's product, even when there is not much of a product to support. Members of these teams are able to project the image of a winning team to top management. They extol the virtues of the team's product and make impressive presentations of what the team can produce. And top management often mirrors what team members tell them and proceeds to spread the positive word to the rest of the organization.

But sometimes these teams are more like "sizzle without the steak." They excel at marketing but do not come through on implementation. In fact, sometimes teams do not seek out top management's support until they are in trouble. Eventually, however, the real story comes out. Then top managers begin to realize that the team made empty promises. Unfortunately, the outcomes for these teams are often quite negative. Top managers are left feeling manipulated and as if they were not given the real story. They are often embarrassed about having backed a team that they thought was creating a real contribution to the firm, only to find that this was not the case. And yet they had made the case to others and put their own reputations on the line. These managers then react in anger and fire, demote, or transfer key members of these teams.

The core lesson here is that ambassadorship alone, with nothing to support it, is like a smoke-and-mirrors show that will eventually be exposed for the fraud that it is. Ambassadorship works well only when teams are managed soundly and tasks are accomplished well—and when ambassadorship accompanies scouting and task coordination.

## Task Coordination

For the Big Bank team, selling communications systems to businesses would involve a fairly complicated set of steps. The team would have to meet with customers to understand their needs; create a solution that matched those needs with the technology that the firm had to offer; bid for the contract when there were other competing vendors; configure a solution if the bid was accepted; and then install the system at the customer's premises.

Succeeding at all of these stages meant team members needed to rely on the input and cooperation of lots of other individuals and groups inside and outside the firm. In other words, what the Big Bank team had to deal with was task coordination. For example, at the very start of the process, team members often needed the help of the legal department to create special clauses in the contract. Sometimes the customer's firm had its own set of contractual terms that needed to be checked against company policy and for their acceptability to the legal team. The Big Bank team wanted to make the sale. The legal group was often very cautious and wanted to spend more time dotting the i's and crossing the t's. It often took a lot of compromise between the two to make timely progress.

The Big Bank team also needed help from technical services to design the system that would be shown to the customer. While the team received some technical support from their colleague Robert, the systems designer, when customers needed communications systems that were very complex or required new configurations that Robert did not understand, Big Bank needed help from the technical support people. Sometimes these people were the only ones who fully understood the new systems, and so they would also be needed to talk to the customer or at least to the technical people within the customer organization. The technical people were often in high demand. They liked to work on interesting problems. Gaining their attention and input was not always easy.

Once a system was designed, it needed to be configured and installed. There was a whole unit, separate from the sales unit, that handled installations. These people had their own set of incentives and cued orders in a way that was most efficient for them. This did not always result in a delivery date that would land a major product at the customer site when the sales team wanted it to be there. There was a need to negotiate.

All of this is to say that members of the Big Bank team had to spend a great deal of their time managing the myriad interdependencies with other parts of the organization. They needed to negotiate with other groups, trade their services, and get feedback on how well their work met expectations. They had to cajole and push other groups to follow through on commitments so that the team could meet its deadlines and keep the work flowing. Like scouting, task coordination involves linking to people throughout the company. It involves lateral and downward connections. But task coordination is much more focused than scouting. The goal is not to learn but to coordinate, align, and motivate cooperation.

Effective teams like Big Bank spend a lot of time trying to figure out how best to garner these other groups' cooperation. Members strategize about how to motivate the installation people to get the order in on time. At one point this team's members were ready to celebrate a big sale when the news came in that the installation group was forecasting a date of December 10 when the customer needed the product by November 17. The Big Bank team knew that this would not be acceptable to the customer, who wanted the system installed before the holiday rush. Luckily, Randy tracked down someone in installation, and he and Russell started to cajole, plead, and bargain. They offered to help with the actual installation if the date could be moved, and they brought in pizza when the installation team had to work late on a Big Bank job. They also offered to trade another installation date that was less important to make the November 17 date. In short, they did whatever it took to keep other groups aligned with their team's interests.

Meanwhile, other teams in the same company shied away from the kind of task coordination activity that Big Bank employed. After all, in the old world you didn't have to talk to "those people in installation," and nobody wanted to start now. It was also countercultural to cross boundaries, and many sales team personnel did not have contacts in these other areas. While this did not stop the Big Bank team, it took a lot of initiative and guts to approach these folks, and not everyone was willing to take on the extra work. In fact, for many teams it was easier to blame their inability to sell on other groups: legal was too conservative, and the installation team never came through. That is precisely how teams avoided taking responsibility for poor results and traveling outside their comfort zone. The only trouble was that members of the Big Bank team had very large bonuses at the end of the year; other teams' members did not. What's more, members of the Big Bank team helped shape the future direction of BellCo—and went on to more prominent positions in the organization.

Let's take a closer look at the three key activities of task coordination: identifying dependencies; getting feedback from other groups; and convincing, negotiating, and cajoling other groups inside and outside the firm to help the team get the task done.

### Identifying Dependencies

The first step in task coordination is identifying the myriad groups that the team must depend on.[12] Such dependencies occur when the other group has something that the team needs to do its work, such as expertise. Or a dependency might arise when another group is going to take over the team's work when it finishes or when someone from that other group is going to join the team to facilitate an aspect of the work. The Big Bank team depended on installation, legal, and repair, to name a few.

Once a dependency is identified, the second step is to determine the nature of the dependency and then figure out a way to coordinate. Coordination can take the form of shared deadlines, ongoing discussions about how the two groups might work together, or mechanisms to move work from one group to the other and back again. Whatever the mode, teams often need to spend a great deal of time managing the work flow in and out of the team.

### Getting Feedback

Coordination is often facilitated when team members get feedback from other groups on what they are planning to do. To the extent that the team's work will affect these other groups, or other groups will expect to be involved in the team's effort, this work becomes even more important. This activity also concentrates more of the organization's resources on the team's work—at least for some time—thus ensuring an improved outcome. For example, when a brainstorming team at IDEO wants creative ideas, they bring in lots of employees who are not core team members but who have broad expertise. These people help the brainstorming become more out of the box, and they can help critique ideas and give feedback from different vantage points, thus improving the ultimate solution.

The product development team mentioned earlier that was working on a revolutionary computer design started its work in isolation. But before the design was written in stone, the team knew it needed some input from colleagues if it hoped to coordinate its plans with other groups. (Note, however, that this kind of coordination is different from the scouting that the team engaged in earlier in the process, when it sought other groups' input for the purpose of avoiding a flawed design.)

The team checked that particular people in R&D could live with the team's decisions and would be willing to commit to their part of the project work. With this input in mind, team members went back to their design work—but now they frequently consulted with other engineers who had provided them with ideas and critiques. This continuous feedback helped them improve their design and coordinate their work with others who were working on specific pieces of the design. The team went on to get feedback from manufacturing, the folks who would actually make the new computer. Team members wanted feedback on the ease of manufacturing the new components that they wanted to put into the machine. If manufacturing thought that this would impede getting the product out on time, then other components might have to be used.

### Convincing, Negotiating, and Cajoling

Perhaps the appropriate heading here would be "begging, borrowing, and beguiling." So often outside groups have other agendas, incentives, and priorities. They are not particularly concerned with the team's needs, and even if they are, they're not always clear on how to meet those needs. Sometimes the functional boundaries and divergent cultures within the firm act as a barrier to cooperation. And so the team must work to make sure the needed cooperation is forthcoming.

The Big Bank team knew that one of its new banking customers was not happy with the product—and that the bank was in fact looking at other companies for its next purchase. Since Big Bank didn't want to lose this account, team members went on a major campaign. They got the technical folks to put a demo together and brought it to the bank. They pushed for a major discount even though it was not yet the end of the quarter. They even got one of their other customers to call the bank manager who made key purchasing decisions to tell him how pleased he was with his system and why. For Vicki, Jean-Yves, Randy, Russell, and Robert, it was a very busy time. They were constantly in touch with all the other groups to make sure that everyone would show up when they said they would and would deliver on all the other commitments. On the day of the demo, they hired a minivan and drove the technical folks across town. They worked hard to pull everyone together. And they kept the customer.

As we've seen, then, team effectiveness is not just a matter of managing well around the conference table. Success also depends on teams' reaching out across their borders to find needed information and expertise. Teams need to access information about key trends in the industry, markets, and technology; link to the firm's strategic goals; survive the power and politics; get buy-in for their product; and manage their dependencies on other groups. Through these activities X-teams practice distributed leadership—working with others in the company to shape new visions and make them a reality. Sometimes X-teams take the lead in shaping strategy, and sometimes they give definition to plans made by others. In either case X-teams help convert leadership from a concept to action. All of this involves the teams' becoming very adept at managing across their boundaries.

And yet, as we will show, large amounts of external activity require effective *internal* processes as well. Extreme execution inside is needed to coordinate the team's external forays, to strategize about how to deal with the new information that comes into the team, and to allocate work to the most appropriate members. Externally oriented teams need a climate of safety and reflection that enables them to hold together the team members who must deal with the pulls of external viewpoints and internal conflict.

Thus, as we have already begun to show in this book, the key to high team performance is an *integrated approach*—combining an external and internal focus. That requires scouting, ambassadorship, and task coordination coupled with extreme execution within, which is the focus of our next chapter.

# FOUR

# X-Team Principle 2

## *Extreme Execution*

W HEN GERHARD KOEPKE, a project manager at the international electrical engineering firm Powercorp, was
sent to an Asian country to set up a manufacturing plant, he was nervous.[1] He had a big job to do, although much was accomplished already.
Gerhard and his business development team had scanned and analyzed
the competitive landscape, producing an impressive investment proposal.
Then they had successfully reached out to top management back in Eu-
rope to sell it. Nevertheless, Gerhard was nervous because he did not
know much about the local regulatory environment in which he was to
get the project off the ground. He decided to invite new members to join
the team who had specific local knowledge. Hoping they could enlighten
him, Gerhard called a team meeting.

During the meeting, everyone assured him that the proposed plan
would work. No regulatory concerns were raised, and Gerhard left the
meeting feeling relieved. But six months later the plant was in the red
with no clear path to profitability. It turned out that though the original

plan called for using a cheap outside source of materials, the country's laws stipulated the use of substantial local sourcing, which was prohibitively more expensive than what Gerhard had budgeted for.

The problem was that no one on Gerhard's team had shared that key bit of national regulatory information, even though several team members had done enough scouting to be well acquainted with the regulations at the time of the first team meeting. They had simply felt too unsure about how to interact with their new foreign boss to speak up. For his part, Gerhard charged forward after that initial meeting, operating on limited knowledge and without thinking more on the matter or fostering further reflection about the sourcing issue, or other potential stumbling blocks, in his team—until it became an irreparable problem. Partly because of the initial underbudgeted costs for critical material, the plant never reached profitability and was sold two years later.

What exactly went wrong here? After all, the team made all the right moves in the business development phase—engaging successfully in numerous external activities. On the surface, this could look like a simple case of miscommunication, common whenever a team is introduced to a new team leader, and particularly common in the kind of cross-cultural context in which Gerhard and his team were operating. And while there were indeed some of these factors at play, they were part of a larger story of internal issues with Gerhard's team that produced such a disappointing outcome for Powercorp.

In light of the exceeding importance of external activities that we just looked at in the last chapter, one might think that the internal activities for a team like Gerhard's would be less important. Think again. An X-team's role in the distributed leadership of the organization includes practicing such leadership within the team itself. When team members were silent about what they knew, they did not take on a leadership role but abdicated this responsibility. Gerhard, for his part, did not create the conditions needed for people to feel safe and reveal the information that the team needed.

All of this is to say that the significance of external activities has possibly made the internal part of the story even more important—and more difficult. If team members spend considerable time and effort on external scouting, ambassadorship, and task coordination, then it becomes a more critical job to integrate the products of these efforts than when most of what the team needs exists in the team from the outset. With more information and demands from the outside come more complicated trade-offs to assess and more difficult decisions to make. When divergent political interests enter the team, those external conflicts can become internal team conflicts. This puts extreme demands on internal coordination and execution. These tasks need to be taken on and shared by members of the team. We refer to this part of the challenge for teams as "extreme execution." This leads to the second of our three X-team principles: *X-teams combine high levels of external activity outside the team with extreme execution inside the team.*

Later in this chapter we'll examine specific tools that foster such seamless execution in teams. But tools only can be used effectively when a team has a healthy culture of interaction.

## A Safe Culture for Extreme Execution

Returning now to our Big Bank team introduced in the last chapter, we see that in addition to great external activity, the team's members also interacted well with each other. When the team was first formed, and the inclination of the members was to do nothing and wait for directives from top management, Vicki stepped in and suggested that they get started figuring out the expectations of key stakeholders and methods of working with outside groups. The team discussed how they would do this over drinks in a local bar. This activity set the tone for the team—be active, coordinate and divide up work, listen to everyone's ideas, and relax and have a good time while working. By organizing themselves and working together, team members were able to conquer their anxiety about their new task, gain confidence about themselves as an effective team, and learn to appreciate the input of all team members.

Later, as information began to pour in, team members pulled it together and interpreted what it meant, while simultaneously inventing new ways of working together inside the team and externally with outsiders. When top management support was won, the team celebrated, and internal motivation and bonding were accelerated. Thus, internal activity and external activity were complementary—the safe and reflective culture inside the team gave members the courage and tools to explore externally and to make good use of the information and expertise that they found. In turn, the time engaged in scouting, ambassadorship, and task coordination gave the team new ideas for innovation, motivation to succeed, and a set of partners to help do the work.

Three fundamental concepts underlie the kind of culture that Big Bank clearly achieved—and that Gerhard's Asian team lacked: psychological safety, team reflection, and knowing what others know.

### Psychological Safety

When team members spend time carrying out the hard work we illustrated in the last chapter—engaged in activities outside the team—they need to work equally hard to coordinate and integrate the fruits of that labor *inside* the team. For team members to share their experiences and express their views of how to move forward, the team's culture must support a frank exchange of views. Such "psychological safety" means that all members feel the team is safe for interpersonal risk taking.[2] It means that team members feel free to express their views, even controversial ones. It means they can bring up problems without fear of being blamed, or worse, being fired. It means they don't think twice about sharing news, even if it is bad news. It means they can voice doubts, even if they're not entirely sure that the doubts are warranted, and it means they can share experiences, even when it is as yet unclear how those experiences might be applicable.

A team with psychological safety is characterized by free-wheeling discussion, which may even involve conflict and a "good fight." More important, it sets the stage for sharing vital information, identifying what matters, and learning from mistakes. From a distributed leadership perspective, the internal team dynamics mirror the very activities that teams need to bring to the larger organization and that the organization needs to support throughout the firm.

At Toyota, for example, when a new car comes off the assembly line with a defective door handle, the person responsible for that part does not fix the problem quietly without the assembly team leader noticing. Instead, the team comes together to identify the root cause of the problem to ensure that it does not happen again.[3] This process often gets noisy, and it requires psychological safety. Without it, quiet fixers would rule the day—leaving the source of the problem and its consequences to crop up again and again. Another example is Southwest Airlines. Consistently profitable in a notoriously unprofitable industry, Southwest's success has, at least in part, been attributed to a culture in which ground crew teams feel free to talk about their own mistakes and those of others without fear of punishment.[4]

In the Big Bank team there was often discussion about mistakes that were made. And there were a lot of them; after all, the team had to learn many new skills and approaches to their new task. During the first few months of its existence, the team was trying to put together a basic sales pitch for the banking industry. At one customer presentation Jean-Yves presented the data about how much better BellCo's system would work vis-à-vis the competition's. Luckily, Big Bank did not win the bid because, as it turned out, the data was incorrect. When the error was discovered, team members set out to figure out how to redo their calculations to get an accurate result, not to figure out who had made the mistake in the first place. Ideas poured out from everyone as members tried to develop a system that would yield the right numbers, rather than dwelling on what had gone wrong. They also celebrated the fact that they had not won the bid and been stuck having to explain incorrect data—they decided that luck was on their side but they better not count on it happening again.

A study of hospital patient-care teams provides some further detail of the importance of psychological safety.[5] The study showed great differences in team members' beliefs about the consequences of reporting errors in medication. In some teams members acknowledged errors openly, while in others they kept such errors to themselves. Moreover, such beliefs tend to be taken for granted ("this is how things are around here"). A nurse in one of the studied teams observed, "Mistakes are serious, because of the toxicity of the drugs [we use]—so you're never afraid to tell the nurse manager." Contrast this with the view of a nurse in a different team: "You get put on trial! People get blamed for mistakes . . . [Y]ou don't want to have made one." The study made an important observation: in teams where errors were acknowledged, ways of avoiding further errors were discussed. This did not happen in teams where errors were not acknowledged.

Yet another example comes from Team EcoInternet, one of the leading teams in adventure racing, a sport that combines paddling, biking, climbing, running, and hiking through the wilderness.[6] In adventure racing, teams of four to five people race across deserts, mountains, and jungles with no more than a map and a compass. For a team to win, it must be a complete team. All team members must be athletic, of course, but that is not enough. This is a team sport in the truest sense of the word. The winner is the team that gets every team member across the finish line first. In other words, having a few star athletes in your team is nice, but not a critical success factor. What is critical is that team members help each other cross the finish line as a team. Therefore, psychological safety is paramount. It means letting go of machismo. It means admitting one's weaknesses and having even the strongest members asking for help when it is needed. It means that all members are celebrated for what they bring to the team—even as each member tries to improve both individually and as a part of the team. This presents a challenge, since few athletes—who are typically fiercely competitive—would readily admit that they need help. According to Robert Nagle, one of EcoInternet's members, the secret to their success is this: "We practice asking for help. We're all really good athletes in our own right, and we've had long, successful careers. But we're all able to make that switch and say, '[I]n order for the team to move faster, I should ask for help.'"

In teams without psychological safety, by contrast, members keep information to themselves. They are hesitant to share it since they feel it may not be seen as important by other team members or it may not be consistent with other members' preconceived notions. They don't ask for help when they need it. They may be scared that they will be labeled as troublemakers or seen as stupid or weak. Or perhaps they do not think it is their place to rock the boat. When information is shared in a team without psychological safety, a far too rare occurrence, it tends to be done privately or offline. The effect is that critical knowledge may not be revealed, processed, or used. Research shows that team members are often more likely to share information that others already have rather than information that they alone have obtained.[7] In a team without psychological safety, this tendency is reinforced, and the team often loses the unique and critical knowledge of individual members.

Clearly, our example of the Asian team at the start of the chapter had just such an issue. For many reasons that came together in one ineffective meeting—not the least of which was that team members felt a little afraid of their new boss—the team did not feel psychologically safe enough to share crucial information about national laws. The information would have changed Gerhard's game plan for the plant, yes—but it might also have saved it.

While we acknowledge that the concept of psychological safety may sound a bit squishy and intangible, both the means to get there and the effects it has on a team involve some very tangible elements. The team leader plays an important role, such as setting explicit norms that encourage members to say what they really think and to express doubts. Encouraging members to "practice asking for help," like Team EcoInternet, may be helpful. Modeling this same behavior herself, the team leader can set an example. Furthermore, when a team leader goes to bat for the team in arguments with external stakeholders and engages in effective ambassadorial activity, he strengthens the psychological safety of the team. Having the confidence that the team leader will stand up for them outside the team promotes members' willingness to take risks inside the team.

At times, encouraging psychological safety may mean recognizing when to get out of the way and let others take the lead. When the head of GE's aircraft engine division, Lorraine Bolsinger, called a series of team meetings to figure out how to deliver on Immelt's "imagination breakthrough" vision, she barred herself from the first few meetings. Since the purpose of those meetings was brainstorming, she wanted to make sure that members were not afraid to feel silly in front of their boss.[8] She also wanted to make sure that all members developed a sense that they, too, were leaders who owned the solution.

Perhaps the most important thing that a formal leader can do is to react positively when team members make points that disagree with her own, or to bring in new perspectives that may seem strange or controversial. If disagreement is punished, then it will surely not be seen very often. Ultimately, psychological safety relies heavily on trust—a commodity that requires consistent nurturing over time. This is the job not only of the formal team leader but of the entire team, which must often take on leadership roles.

### Team Reflection

A second component of a culture of extreme execution is team reflection.[9] That is, team members need to take the time to reflect on their actions, strategies, and objectives. Without reflection, team members cannot learn what they are doing right and what they are doing wrong. In a world of changing technologies, markets, and high levels of competition, team members also need to reflect on what is changing and whether they need to adapt to those changes. A culture of extreme execution requires learning as you go, and team reflection helps the team keep this learning a priority. In many of today's corporations, there is a push for continuous action; team reflection helps team members pause and make sure that their action is aimed in the right direction. Such reflective pauses are particularly important at key points in the process—at the beginning, the midpoint, and the end of a team's task. At the beginning and midpoint, the team is likely to face strategic decisions that will launch them on a long-term trajectory. These are also times when the team is most open to feedback—when teams make a switch from automatically performing tasks to consciously processing the information involved in doing new tasks. Reflection as the team changes phases of work also aligns team learning with moments when members are open to feedback and change.[10] Reflection at the end of the project helps the team learn important lessons that can then be recorded and carried forward to other teams after it has concluded its work and disbanded.

Members of a team characterized by a high level of reflection often ask questions and seek feedback, and make adjustments in response to that feedback. Such a team has an orientation toward learning. Whenever possible, team members do this together and face-to-face as a team, not offline. A team characterized by high levels of reflection is likely to have highly effective debriefings. Specifically, team members meet to debrief after the completion of a task, at the midpoint, or at key milestones along the way to talk about what worked and what didn't, and to analyze the role that each person played in the successes and failures of that mission.

But truly reflective teams go well beyond debriefings. Members set aside time to think about the big picture, where the team is going, and how things can be done better; and they lean on each other in that effort.

This means going beyond learning about what went well and what went poorly. It means asking deeper questions like: What does the team want to achieve, really? Is the team moving in that direction? Are members truly working on the things that they have pegged as the highest priorities? Can the team move away from the day-to-day to discuss its vision for the long term and how to get there? Are members working well together as a team, or do things need to change? If so, how? Reflection is also a time to make sense of all the information and knowledge collected from the outside and to determine what it all means—and what it means for the team.

The Toyota assembly team that takes time to figure out the root cause of a defect is one example of a reflective team in action. And it's important that team members take this time even though it might not always be possible in the midst of completing a task. The EcoInternet team, for instance, does not have time to reevaluate a decision once it has been made as long as the race is going on, even if it turns out to be a bad decision. Robert Nagle, the EcoInternet member mentioned earlier, explains: "You have to treat mistakes as the next challenge, rather than as a self-inflicted problem. So we tend to say, 'OK, we decided to come over this ridge instead of following the valley around. It's worse than we expected. But that doesn't matter. We just have to deal with the circumstances and move on.'" This makes the debriefing afterward all the more important. "We come back after each race and analyze every decision in a very honest and pretty raw fashion," says Nagle. "We talk about why people acted the way they did, why we made particular decisions, and how we ended up in particular circumstances."

Team Fox members had frequent debriefings about how the process was going, but they also took time to reflect on where they were going at key points. For example, as the team identified and evaluated promising early-stage drugs, they also needed to stop and look at the big picture: the ambition of building a franchise in anti-inflammatory drugs. In at least one instance this led the team to reluctantly let go of a promising lead early on. While the drug performed well in initial tests, in the end, the team members concluded that it did not fit the vision and the direction that the team had agreed on.

Members of a team characterized by a low level of reflection, on the other hand, tend to act on what they already know, whether or not there are alternative solutions out there. They tend not to seek feedback or be concerned with changing circumstances, and when they ask questions, it is typically to confirm what they already know, rather than to explore what they may not know. That seemed to be a tendency in Gerhard's Powercorp team. Whether or not Gerhard intended to encourage this behavior, the team showed an orientation toward uncertainty avoidance—which effectively precludes substantive learning—often in the name of efficiency. Unfortunately, the result may be that the team learns to do the wrong things right. Had Gerhard helped team members to feel psychologically safe and encouraged them to openly express doubts, to bring up all possible high-risk problems, and to then reflect on whether they had done so, he might have discovered the local sourcing problem, and thus, members might have had a chance to avoid a situation in which high material costs rendered their venture unprofitable.

Contrast the Powercorp team with Team Fox, which keenly reflected at critical times on its internal process and direction—what worked, what didn't work, what could be improved, where they were going and why. Had it not done so, it may have ended up developing a drug that no one needed or that wouldn't pass the regulatory requirements. Or the team may have ended up with a drug that was good but did not fit the larger vision of Pharmaco.

How can team reflection be cultivated? Just as with fostering psychological safety, reflection requires that formal team leaders make a commitment to cultivating it (in fact, creating psychological safety is in itself a powerful promoter of team reflection). One way is to build in time to reflect by using check-ins at the beginning of each team meeting and check-outs at the end, to see what members have on their mind and also to set a process in which everyone in the team speaks.[11]

For Team Fox, frank reflection of this sort early in the process had an important impact. During such team discussion, a junior team member drew the team's attention to potential problems with an early-stage drug that was originally considered a very good prospect. The data from the animal tests looked a bit strange to this team member, and once the issue was brought to the attention of the others, it was quickly discovered that the scales used to present important test results were inconsistent. In the process of presenting the materials to different audiences, the inventor of the drug had mixed up different kinds of data. Once necessary recalculations were made, it was clear to the team that the results did not pass muster and that this small error might have had costly consequences. Instead, the team discarded this early lead and continued to search for better alternatives.

Another way to promote team reflection might be by scheduling an off-site day with the entire team, devoted to reflecting on the team's progress in a fundamental way. Typically, such venues are used to reflect more in depth on what's happening in the team, and indeed the change of scenery and relaxed atmosphere can generate new levels of discussion about the norms of the team and its strategies for getting the job done. As part of this effort, team members can be encouraged to talk about the best and the worst experiences they have had and about how to improve team experiences overall.

### Knowing What Others Know

The third element of building a culture of extreme execution is creating a shared sense of what others in the team know. When engaged in complex tasks involving advanced knowledge—such as the development of a new drug, a new car, or a new software product—team members often bring highly specialized skills to the table. Many individual team members possess knowledge that is critical to the task but not shared with others on the team. Therefore, to integrate the different skill sets represented on the team and to complete the task successfully, team members need to know not only their own area of expertise but also other team members' areas of expertise. (These skills, by the way, need not be highly advanced technical skills. Often the most important skill is knowing key people outside the team, and sometimes it may be a more common skill, such as knowing how to prepare a slideshow.) Members of a team who are advanced in this area know their own area of expertise as well as what other team members know, and they have well-developed lines of communication to access the expertise of other team members when needed.[12]

Knowing what others know enables a team to connect islands of expertise into a system in which the right members work on the right tasks at the right time. It also enables team members to know whom to turn to when there is something they do not know and to distribute leadership tasks. Combining knowing what others know with psychological safety and team reflection creates a powerful culture for capitalizing on tools for extreme execution.

It's important to understand that, in a team with members who know what others know, the sum of the members' expertise is greater than its parts. A simple story about the experience of one Team Fox member serves to illustrate this point. The member, responsible for clinical tests, was a top-notch scientist who knew exactly what needed to be done. The problem was that he needed additional data to do it—information related to the drug's safety—and he did not know where to find it. Another team member, meanwhile, who was responsible for basic research, had no idea about *how* to assess the drug's safety. Nor did she know *what* information was required. But a conversation with the first team members uncovered that she did know *where* to find the required information. Specifically, she knew of another team that had recently worked on a similar drug that had the needed data set readily available. In other words, one team member knew what needed to be done but not where to find the information needed to do it. Another member did not know what needed to be done, or even what needed to be known, but did know where to find the required information. Together they were able to accomplish what neither of them could have done on their own, and knowing what others know was the key to this important result. This may seem to be a trivial example. When multiplied, however, these kinds of connections between team members create a mosaic of connections that constitutes knowing what others know at work—with powerful effects on team performance.

On the other hand, as we saw with Powercorp, a team that doesn't have in place a norm of knowing what others know breeds ineffectiveness—and worse. The Powercorp team members didn't share critical knowledge about the country's regulatory laws—to the team's peril and eventual demise.

The Big Bank team members, however, knew what other people knew and also shared their information. It was clear that Vicki and Jean-Yves, as the salespeople, knew most about sales, about the banking industry, and, due to intense scouting, about the banking customers and what their needs were. Randy and Russell knew most about how to configure the systems, and later they also came to know most about the sign-off process within the customer companies. This knowledge would help the team complete the sale. Robert knew most about how to solve the difficult design problems and how to work with the technology staff from the customer sites to work out glitches in implementation.

But beyond their knowledge specialties, these team members also knew a lot about each other. They knew that Vicki was not a morning person and preferred team meetings later in the day. They knew that Jean-Yves had more of an international background and thus would often lead the sales presentation with an international client. They knew that Randy had a side interest in law and was a great liaison to the legal team, while Russell was more of a business type and was good at coming up with creative ideas for negotiating the final agreement. Robert, on the other hand, did not care much for any of this. Give him an interesting technical problem, and he was happy. All of this knowledge helped the team give work to the people who were most competent and would enjoy it the most. When these demands could not be accommodated, the team had a culture of joking around and asking whether success was possible with idiots doing the work. The response was usually something like, "Be careful, I might do a better job than you did."

But how do you go about making sure the team is one in which everyone knows what the others know? First, you staff the team with members whose expertise, when combined, covers critical knowledge areas and then make sure everyone on the team knows what everyone else knows. The latter is important to accomplish early on in a team meeting or an off-site retreat devoted to mapping the team's expertise. Questions to ask members may include: What do you know? Whom do you know? How is it important to the task? What other team experiences have you had? In what kinds of projects have you worked, and what did you learn? What don't you know? Does anyone else in the team know this or where to find someone who knows? Hence, in such a meeting members need to talk about what expertise each of them brings to the team. This is more than just knowledge about a certain subject, such as manufacturing or marketing, although that is critical. It is also about the networks that members bring to the team, such as external experts and political connections. Furthermore, it is important to figure out what each person likes to do or would like to develop—for example, conducting research, interviewing, analyzing data, making presentations, and so on. The result should be a map of the different tasks to be done and who should be doing them.

This is just a start, however. The procedure may need to be repeated as the process unfolds and for specific tasks. Otherwise, knowing what others know risks becoming too abstract. So whenever the team encounters a new step, it is helpful to ask questions specific to the new context:

Does anyone know anything about this particular step? If not, do you know of anyone who does? So for each step and each juncture, the questions may have to be repeated, and expertise and preferences may need to be shared again.

Key to developing all three areas we've discussed so far in this chapter—psychological safety, team reflection, and knowing what others know—is understanding that none of these elements operates very well in isolation. The goal is to work toward an iterative, circular process: knowing what others know is promoted by team reflection. Team reflection is facilitated by psychological safety, which in turn is strengthened by knowing what others know. The three building blocks of a culture of extreme execution constitutes an internally consistent system—which sets the stage for the next step in your team's internal process: using the tools for extreme execution.

## Tools for Extreme Execution

Creating a team in which extreme execution is the norm begins by ensuring that the culture itself reflects that norm, but specific tools can help. Five tools in particular work well to achieve coordination and execution in X-teams: integrative meetings, participatory and transparent decision-making procedures, heuristics, shared timelines, and information management systems.

### Integrative Meetings

One of the best ways to bring about consistent team reflection and to actively hone knowing what others know is through integrative meetings. An institutionalized, frequent meeting of core team members, the integrative meeting is a war room for sharing what team members have found and gauging progress against the major tasks, goals, and milestones set by them. Any meeting can be used as an opportunity for integration.

Although such meetings are typically held at the end of major milestones, the team process should be flexible enough to allow for more improvised ones at short notice, if needed. Through these meetings, team members share their knowledge and views and also the information and experiences they have obtained through external activity. That helps keep everyone informed and increases the information's value by making it widely available. The meetings ensure that decisions are based on real-time data from combinations of scouting, ambassadorship, and task coordination. Without such meetings, adaptation to changing conditions is much more difficult.

The Big Bank team had many integrative meetings. Some took place at the office, some at the local bar, and some while traveling to and from customer sites. Team members took advantage of time together to delegate tasks and plan responses to events in the field. Early on, team members often broke up a task depending on people's task specialties: the salespeople (Vicki and Jean-Yves) took on the scouting tasks associated with learning about banking and systems selling, and the more technical members (Robert, Randy, and Russell) were assigned to work with the other technical groups in the organization and the people that the Big Bank team would be working with as orders started coming in. Vicki, the formal team leader, was assigned most of the interaction with top management. Extreme execution during integrative meetings inside was needed to best allocate resources to engage in external activity outside.

Later, meetings would include "report-outs" from each member about key learnings from these discussions. Together the team members worked to pull this information into a map of how they would interact with other groups. They also used these meetings to brainstorm about how to best attract important customers. It was not enough to engage in external activity. If that activity did not result in team members' bringing in disparate information and converting that into knowledge, new procedures, and better ways to work in the future, then it was wasted activity.

A team at BP also illustrates the power of integrative meetings. Charged with examining how to improve project management practices for large complex projects at the energy firm, the team faced some serious hurdles right from the start. Not only did the six team members span five time zones, making coordination a cumbersome task, but in addition to working on this task, they had full-time jobs. The team decided to deal with this coordination challenge in part by dividing the work into clearly defined tasks. For example, they broke up the scouting work by having one member look at past project successes, and another at past failures. A third team member interviewed three members of the top management group to get their sense of the problem, while two others looked at best practices in other companies. The breadth and depth of scouting activities yielded extensive results—case studies of what others were doing, interview transcripts, and so on—and the data was all shared among team members.

Still, they felt stuck. It was only after the members finally met in a face-to-face integrative meeting that things changed, issues were resolved, and real progress was made. It was only in this meeting that members could discuss in depth what all the information they had collected really meant. They could now wrestle in earnest with some key questions: How did the pieces fit together? What would the team's next steps be? Did the team need more data? Could existing data be broken down into common themes? If so, what were those themes? What would a presentation of the project to top management three weeks later look like? The team members came to understand that one of the problems was that people in the organization used the same words to mean different things. They also found three core themes that were true across the data sources in terms of what differentiated high-performing and low-performing projects. But all of this took discussion and conversation in the forum of the integrative meeting.

Similarly, the Razr team at Motorola had to resolve a series of tricky technical issues before launching its new phone, such as the placement of the antenna. Roger Jellicoe, the formal team leader, often found that team members had collected a pallet of ideas in their discussions with various external experts that were promising but not really useful when considered separately. He then put together a sketch based on the various ideas and called a meeting. He explains the process: "None of those ideas was the complete solution, and so the tradeoffs or risks were judged unacceptable when each was considered separately. When novel ideas were put together, however, the risks seemed manageable. This illustrates both the hazards of group thinking and the fact that innovation can sometimes move forward only when ideas are evaluated in combination rather than in isolation."[13] Such "evaluation in combination" is the hallmark of an effective integrative meeting.

Integrative meetings can have their problems, however. For global teams separated by long distances, such as the team at BP, managing integrative meetings can be quite difficult, and such teams will have to rely more on electronic coordination. Even in these cases, however, we have found it helpful to have periodic meetings via satellite link—although this might mean that one person is in at 1 a.m., another at 7 a.m., and yet another at 6 p.m.

Integrative meetings could also potentially compromise efficiency, slowing down the team process. Team Fox used a simple rule to manage this problem: "No one has to sit through an entire meeting." In practice, this meant that different parts of the team came only to the portion of the meeting most relevant to them. Of course, having people popping in and out of meetings can be quite disruptive. This idea, therefore, should be applied with common sense. Nonetheless, when practiced in moderation, it can be an effective rule of thumb.

### *Participatory and Transparent Decision-Making Procedures*

Psychological safety, team reflection, and knowing what others know sets the stage for effective decision making—if the procedures are participatory. Participatory and transparent decision making, which gives members a say and keeps them informed about the reasons behind choices, is good for nudging everyone in the same direction and for maintaining motivation. "Even when I have an idea or a plan, I try to invite people to be part of the problem solving," says a team leader at Industrial Light & Magic, a Hollywood special-effects firm. "That way, they feel like part of the team—and they usually come up with a better idea than mine."[14]

Even when team members are frustrated that something they have worked on has been dropped, they appreciate knowing about the change and why it has been made. This is particularly important when team members spend significant time on external activity and key information on which decisions are based comes from an array of external sources.

Participatory decision making proved important for the Razr team at Motorola. In fact, many of the solutions selected for the Razr phone were picked from competing solutions suggested by various members of the team. For example, the team had ten different blueprints to evaluate for the tricky issue of the antenna placement. There was intense discussion and many disappointed advocates, but in the end, everyone who had put sweat equity into finding a solution got a say in the final decision. Interestingly, the winning formula—an elegant solution that placed the antenna in the mouthpiece—was proposed by one of the most junior members of the team, a then thirty-two-year-old engineer named Tadd Scarpelli. Razr was capable of taking important decisions based on merit rather than on the seniority of the champion of any given alternative. For truly merit-based decisions, participation of all concerned parties is key.

The Big Bank team had very transparent decision making. At one point Randy and Russell had put a lot of time and energy into designing a system for a potential customer, and they were very proud of their new design. But as negotiations continued, Vicki felt that the team would not be able to make enough money to warrant the amount of time and effort that was needed to put in such a complex system. She also wasn't sure that the company could actually deliver the system Randy and Russell had designed. In the end, she decided not to continue in the bidding process. Randy and Russell were extremely disappointed. They had wanted to go ahead with the new system just to see how it would work and whether it could do the job they thought it could do. But, ultimately, they went along with the decision—they understood that their technological curiosity had to come second to making the numbers and having a satisfied customer. Vicki, however, promised that as they got more experienced configuring systems, they might revisit more complex designs in the future.

### *Heuristics*

When team members engage in external activity, it is important that they are given the mandate to be entrepreneurial. On the other hand, no direction at all spells anarchy. The solution? Heuristics—or rules of thumb—that give guidelines about and boundaries around the process and help team members make decisions when circumstances are ambiguous.[15] For example, the Big Bank team's main heuristic is "the customer comes first"—and teammates all understand what that entails. It means that you push other support teams, you work late hours, and you do all that you can for your key priority: the customer.

We also have mentioned Team Fox's rule of "no one has to sit through an entire meeting." This helped members make decisions about how to use their time most efficiently. Two other heuristics were important as regulators of the process in Team Fox's organization. The first was that the need to obtain sufficient information to make an appropriate evaluation was greater than the need for a speedy process. For example, when a team member saw the opportunity to learn more about running a series of important experiments by visiting a lab at her alma mater, she jumped at it. Time was precious, but she decided that the extra day the expedition would entail should yield benefits that far outweighed the costs of losing some time. She did let the rest of the team know of her trip but did not ask for the formal team leader's view of whether it was appropriate—she knew the team heuristic dictated that it was.

The second heuristic for Team Fox was that the benefits of including more people in the effort were greater than the need for internal control. This was a particularly important issue for Team Fox since the team worked on a drug whose scientific and regulatory underpinnings were not intuitively understood by team members. Hence, the need for external expertise was often acute. On the other hand, the inclusion of more people in the effort could cause confusion and coordination problems. The heuristic helped team members make important decisions fast about bringing in expertise in the face of this difficult trade-off. For example, the team member responsible for reviewing the proprietary position of the drug that Team Fox was working on found that more resources were needed to do background research on international intellectual property laws. To fulfill the need, he simply added two junior lawyers working for the firm as supporting team members. They were available for a brief time, their boss agreed to have them work with Team Fox, and the team member took the opportunity to add the extra competence to the team for part of the project's duration.

An important point is that Team Fox's heuristics were valid unless something else was stated that overrode the guideline in place. In fact, speed and internal control were often very important—and it is not uncommon that teams get stuck in information-gathering mode, which slows down execution. But in case there was no time for team members to visit their alma maters, or if adding more members would make the team too unwieldy, it was up to the formal team leader to say so. This way, team members did not have to deal with ambiguities when it came to their mandate and were able to make quick decisions when needed.

Autonomy combined with rules of thumb enable teams such as Team Fox to work fast. Little time gets wasted waiting for permission. Another firm known for its fast teams is the U.S. consulting firm Cambridge Technology Partners (CTP). Tammy Urban, who was a project manager with the firm in the late 1990s, cites heuristics as key to the fast pace of CTP's teams.[16] For example, CTP had a "two-minute rule" for seeking advice. Says Urban, "When someone was stuck on a problem, we didn't want them to wait more than two minutes to ask for help." In other words, no one should feel any ambiguity about whether asking for another team member's time and help is the right thing to do. Early on, when a team is small, this may simply mean speaking up—which is easy enough as long as the team has the requisite level of psychological safety. As teams at CTP grow, however, internal Web-based discussion lists are used.

### Shared Timelines

Another way to make sure that team members who are engaged in external activity will work smoothly toward the same goal is to provide shared timelines. Flexibility that allows for deadline shifts and adjustments are important, particularly in fast-changing environments. But the key thing is that shared timelines allow members to pace themselves and to coordinate work with others despite spending time away from the team involved in scouting, ambassadorship, and task coordination.

Many members on Team Fox spent considerable time engaged in external activities, which meant that they often were far away from each other physically. Therefore, they could not rely on bumping into each other by the watercooler or coffeemaker, which meant few opportunities for spontaneous coordination. This also meant that it was not realistic to have team meetings as frequently as might have been desirable. Since the project moved quickly, teammates had to find other means of coordination. In particular, team members had clear assignments, and although they had a lot of discretion over how to complete those assignments, they were asked to report electronically to the rest of the team about their weekly progress, say, by 10 a.m. every Friday. Furthermore, there were some deadlines that everyone shared. One particularly important deadline was set for the end of the so-called research phase of the project. At this date all the members responsible for the various scientific disciplines involved would have to have their findings ready to consolidate into a comprehensive report.

Now consider software development teams at Microsoft.[17] Team members are known for setting their own schedules, and they own the features of the product they're developing in the sense that they're fully responsible for coming up with and integrating those features. Since a lot of task coordination is required, however, there are a few important rules of timing. One is that at a particular time every day—say, at 3 p.m.—there is a new "build," which is when partially completed or finished pieces of a software product are integrated with the rest of the code. So even though members are free to come to work whenever they please and to contribute to the product build as frequently or rarely as they like, they're still all forced to synchronize their work. This shared timeline includes an important norm: "Don't break the build." In other words, do not violate the interdependencies between features. Developers responsible for bugs that break the build must fix them immediately—and they must take responsibility for the next day's build or pay an embarrassing fine. Along with Microsoft's 3 p.m. coordinating time comes a heavy use of other shared timelines. The daily update of the build provides a time pacer, but more important, "milestone stabilization" is key. Managers do not care where or when team members work, but to miss intermediate milestone deadlines is considered totally unacceptable.

Discovery Health—a South African health insurance company lauded for innovation in an industry not known for it—has gone even further.[18] Every November, Discovery has a mammoth product launch. The venue for the launch is booked in advance, before there is a product. The use of this timeline is based on the shared understanding in Discovery's management team that it has to reinvent its product line every year. The self-imposed urgency to come up with innovative products by a nonnegotiable date has worked well. At the November 2003 launch, for instance, the Discovery team changed the financing of health care radically and introduced a plan offering comprehensive cover at prices 25 percent below the previous year's rate. A shared timeline, in this case, serves to coordinate the efforts of different members of the management team—who are responsible for different functions and physically dispersed—and to have them work toward the same goal in the same rhythm. It also serves to speed up the process.[19]

### Information Management Systems

Finally, timely and updated information is key for both effective external activity and extreme execution internally. A good information management system gives access to information, know-how, and experts, but it also provides an easy way for team members to feed important information back to the team so that knowledge that comes into the team can be monitored. For instance, as the Fox teammates were scouting for a promising early-stage drug, they were racing against time. Good leads were contested, so a decision on moving forward needed to be made quickly. Yet the information needed to perform a decent evaluation was complex and expansive. Therefore, as soon as a team member uncovered critical data, it was fed back to the team's files in Pharmaco's database. That way, the responsible person could start the analysis right away.

A tracking and planning system that maps key tasks, who is responsible for the tasks, and when the tasks need to be finished can be another key instrument of coordination among team members engaged in external activities. In the case of Team Fox, such a system helped members make important decisions about how to invest their time. For example, if a team member visited a university lab to gain insights on a toxicology profile, that member would know how urgently the data was needed—given the sequential nature of the series of tests a drug has to go through—and who needed it.

DaimlerChrysler has attempted to meet the challenges of increased external team activities in part by developing a sophisticated Internet-based IT platform called FastCar.[20] This allows the car development teams to tap into information flows from a large number of information systems that previously did not communicate seamlessly. Perhaps most important, FastCar facilitates extreme execution and task coordination in car development teams that are typically large and complex. For example, as designers go though hundreds of variations, other functions involved in the development efforts can understand what is changing—in real time. In the past, if designers changed something, engineers would have to catch up later and figure out what the effects might be on manufacturing, and finance would have to reassess the costs. By then, of course, the designers would be working on the next iteration. Therefore, FastCar offers what DaimlerChrysler calls a "single point of truth" for teams. That is, there is one iteration that all members are working on. No team members ever have to ask themselves whether they're working on the latest version. And it's important to note that FastCar is not only aimed at the internal process: the goal is to link up seamlessly with suppliers as well.

Many teams that we know have found something they call a "know-who" database, or expert finder, particularly useful. Hewlett-Packard was one of the first to create this kind of electronic Yellow Pages–like directory of experts inside the firm.[21] These systems can range from simple internal search engines powered by Google to spectacularly advanced proprietary network-based systems. Postmortem team reports and elaborate explanations of how to perform tasks take time to read, and often the lessons learned are too context specific to be translated easily. Says Texaco's John Old, a manager with many years of knowledge management experience at the oil giant: "Many companies create elaborate databases of best practice, which I find tend not to work very well—at least not as a pure database. For example, somebody discovers a nifty way of saving a million bucks and writes up a story for the 'Best Practices' feature in our in-house magazine. Maybe the idea will get used in exactly the same way in another country—but maybe not. Knowledge transfer occurs because the right *people* happen to meet. We view our databases more as indirect pointers to people than as actual ways of sharing specific ideas."[22]

Old recalls a compelling know-who story of a Texaco team member who, when faced with a problem, used PeopleNet—Texaco's expert finder—to contact someone with twenty-five years of drilling experience to help clear up the matter. "The person who needed help was confused over how to figure out the 'pinhole' position on the equipment that controls how far an oil well's pump goes up and down," Old said. The problem was that he was getting contradictory directions. Using PeopleNet, he found who could help. "What I liked most about the story was that the person with the question chose to ask the 25-year veteran because he had read his biography and had seen his picture on the Internet. He wrote that the more experienced person's photograph had made him appear to be a likable guy who wouldn't seem to mind answering a question from a stranger in the company."

Key takeaway? Make your expert-finding system user friendly—and your experts too. It is much easier to go straight to the people who have the experience rather than to sift through information compiled in a different context, attempting to put a square peg in an all-too-round hole. Note too that these systems—whether dedicated to know-who, to integrating knowledge and information, or to tracking and planning key tasks and responsibilities—need not be supersophisticated. Some teams use simple mechanisms like blogs. The point is that, to make such a system work, participants need to be rewarded and acknowledged for taking time to update the information in the system.

We've seen in this chapter how ensuring extreme execution in a team means crafting the kind of culture in which that is likely to happen—and using the tools that foster the internal processes that are needed to coordinate, integrate, and reap the benefits of the external activities of an X-team. In this way the X-team models distributed leadership in action for the rest of the organization. Still, there is another X-team principle we have yet to look at: that the needs and priorities of both a team's external and the internal processes change over time. Next, we will discuss that temporal dimension of an X-team: the importance of flexible phases.

# FIVE

# X-Team Principle 3

## *Flexible Phases*

THE PROPRINT TEAM at a large West Coast computer company was launched with much fanfare. Charged with developing a revolutionary new printer, the team began work with top managers who expressed their hope that the team could take the company in a new direction. ProPrint set out to work with ample financial and personnel resources and six months to "play in the sandbox," experimenting with different technologies and product designs. The work was divided up so that different team members worked on separate aspects of the new design and got input from different parts of the organization and outside world. The team members had a great deal of information about the market potential, the applications for this technology, and how they could put the new product together. The team was very excited and worked long hours, getting as many new ideas as possible on the table.

After nine months, however, team members could still not agree on what exactly the first product was going to do, or what components they were going to use in its design. Their response to being behind schedule was to continue seeking additional ideas and changing the product design. Although top management had been quite lenient early on, eventually it started applying pressure, hoping to get commitments on schedules. Still, the team was always late. During this time the team leader was often hard to find. Always promising that the solution was "coming soon," he avoided meetings with top managers.

In the end, the division manager was forced to put together another team to continue the ProPrint team's work. The manager never did understand why the team could not get past the continuous search and move on to solutions.[1]

How did such a promising team lose its way? It had appeared to be doing everything the best X-teams do. It engaged in high levels of scouting of the market and organizational expectations; ambassadorial activity leading to managerial support; and task coordination so that team members knew how to work with other groups to create the new product. Moreover, the ProPrint team also illustrated extreme execution, whereby team members divided up work and did intense amounts of brainstorming.

The problem was this: the team did not understand that whether a team is creating a new product, suggesting a new organizational process, consulting to a particular geographic region, selling complex products, or writing software code, members need to shift their core focus over time. As the demands of the task change, team members must be flexible enough to shift gears and change what they do and how they do it.[2]

Flexible phases, then, represent the third X-team principle: *X-teams change their core tasks over the team's lifetime*. This ensures that teams don't get stuck in any one mode of operating. More specifically, effective teams move through three phases, each with a different focus: exploration, exploitation, and exportation.

So first, teams need to organize themselves to examine the world around them, think in new directions, and consider multiple possible options (exploration). But then they must choose one direction and organize themselves for effective action and implementation (exploitation). Finally, teams need to take one last step and shift their focus again toward ensuring that their work has traction in the larger organization (exportation).

The point is that team members need to be able to shift away from an emphasis on exploration—thoroughly understanding the product, process, opportunity, or task that the team has undertaken. They need to be able to move on to exploitation—using the information from exploration to innovate and actually make their dreams and ideas into something real—and finally to exportation, in which they transfer team member expertise and enthusiasm to others who will continue the work of the team, bringing the team's product into the organization and possibly the marketplace. Each of these different phases requires a different focus and hence different amounts and kinds of X-team activity.

But for some teams, these transitions seem impossible. Not all teams realize that at some point members must move from exploring the terrain to moving ahead. Not all teams understand that at some point their new idea needs to extend beyond their boundaries and be integrated into ongoing organizational routines. They become stuck in one mode and fail because they are not able to shift into the next one.[3] Like the ProPrint team, members can become so enamored of playing in the sandbox of ideas during exploration that they don't want to ever come out. Or they are waiting for one more piece of data, or one more report, before moving ahead. The problem is that sometimes the move never happens. These teams have members who thrive on viewing the problem in new ways, questioning prior assumptions, and pondering the myriad possible directions that the team can take. This is fine for exploration, but then the team has to move on.

Other teams err by forgetting about exploration altogether and moving immediately into the implementation and action of exploitation. The drive to get things done in these cases is so intense that teams just start with the solution that first comes to mind. Management can sometimes unknowingly emphasize this "solution mindedness" by pushing the team to make tough targets quickly. The trouble here is that members may be moving quickly in the wrong direction or fail to think outside the box. Finally, some teams never want to let go of their product. No one is interested in exportation; no one takes responsibility for easing the product out of the team and into the rest of the organization. Without this transfer of enthusiasm and ownership, team members may find their work rejected or simply ignored.

But why is it so important to move through these phases? From a team point of view, members need to move toward their goals and produce something of value to them and to the organization. Progress builds momentum, pride, and strong bonds within the team; praise from outside bolsters these outcomes and provides recognition and often rewards from management. This progress requires that team members move from ideas to implementation, from something within their own orbit to something of value to the organization. For team members, the X-team also becomes a vehicle for their voices. This is a chance for them to put their own ideas into action and see what happens. If they fail to make something happen, then their voices may never be heard again.

From a competitive standpoint, if the organization is to perform well, it must have a steady stream of innovative products and processes. Innovation comes when team members see the world with new eyes and are open to new possibilities, and then move to rapid prototyping. That's where all the possibilities become realities that can then be tested with customers and users and be improved through feedback. In addition, remaining competitive at this moment in time means working quickly. If teams are stuck for long periods, their window of opportunity might well close as competitors gain first-mover advantage. There's another danger as well: if too much time elapses, then information obtained during exploration becomes dated and the whole process needs to begin anew.

But flexible phases are also important for another key reason: they enable X-teams to engage in distributed leadership as team members work with others in the organization to create an adaptive structure for innovation and change. By moving through these three phases, X-teams are not just talking about distributed leadership; they are engaging in the actions that bring distributed leadership to life and make organizational change an ongoing practice.

Before we launch into a more detailed look at each phase, we want to offer an important insight into how these phases overlap with and inform the sequence of external activities described earlier in the book: scouting, ambassadorship, and task coordination. In general, while those external activities form the basics of X-teams, flexible phases dictate the "sentence structure" or "grammar" by which these basic elements are ordered and combined.

More specifically, scouting occurs in all three phases, but it is highest during exploration. Ambassadorship also occurs in all three phases, but is most important during exploration and exportation. Likewise, tasks are coordinated in each of the phases, but that coordination becomes much more critical as the team moves toward the final phase.

Flexible phases also dictate the sequencing of the four capabilities that are central to distributed leadership in action. These four capabilities include: sensemaking, relating, visioning, and inventing.[4] Sensemaking, a term coined by Karl Weick, refers to understanding the context in which a team and its members operate.[5] Relating develops key relationships within and across organizations. Visioning creates a compelling picture of the future, and inventing designs new ways of working together to realize the vision. Each of the three phases of activity—exploration, exploitation, and exportation—demands a different combination of distributed leadership capabilities. We will explore the four leadership capabilities further in our concluding chapter, as we return to the theme of X-teams as an essential vehicle for distributed leadership in action.

Table 5-1 summarizes the key tasks of each phase and the leadership and team activities that need to occur to successfully move from one phase to the next. Let's look now at each flexible phase in turn, beginning with exploration.

**TABLE 5-1**

## Phases of X-Teams

| | PHASES | | |
|---|---|---|---|
| | **Explore** | **Exploit** | **Export** |
| **Tasks** | Discovery:<br><br>• See the world through new eyes; get inspired; map the context, the issues, the task, the customer, the technology, the individuals involved<br><br>• Create understanding and multiple possibilities<br><br>• Get buy-in from top management | Design:<br><br>• Choose one option and move from ideas to reality<br><br>• Engage in rapid prototyping and search for best practices to hone the product, process, or idea | Diffusion:<br><br>• Create enthusiasm on the part of those who will carry on the work of the team in the organization or the marketplace<br><br>• Get feedback from top management and the customer about how the team has met expectations |
| **Key leadership activities** | • Sensemaking<br><br>• Relating | • Visioning<br><br>• Inventing | • Relating |
| **Core X-team activities** | • Scouting<br><br>• Ambassadorship | • Ambassadorship<br><br>• Task coordination | • Task coordination<br><br>• Ambassadorship |

## Exploration

A team of equity traders from Merrill Lynch with eight to ten years of experience at the firm was charged with designing a new product using cutting-edge ideas about financial risk as outlined by Professor Andrew Lo in an investments course taught at Merrill Lynch by MIT Sloan School of Management faculty.

Coached to take an X-team approach by one of us, team members began by "sensemaking" about their industry. (As we mentioned, sensemaking refers to trying to understand the situation that you are currently facing.) In 2004, financial services were going through tough times: margins were getting compressed, and the business was getting more automated, resulting in more and more cost cuts. In both equities (stocks) and debt (bonds), markets had become too efficient. If word got out that something good was going on at Coca-Cola or Citigroup, everyone joined the feeding frenzy, and there was no way to make a lot of money. This team determined that it wanted to find a place where the market was not so efficient—where there was not so much coverage on the street in terms of research and information.

With this goal in mind, the team went into intense scouting and ambassadorial activity, looking for ideas and buy-in. But team members were not too sure how to go about this. Most of the team members were used to working at their own jobs, making their targets. They were not used to thinking more broadly or reaching out to people they did not know to brainstorm new product ideas. So team members were a bit unclear about what steps to follow.

But deadlines for reporting on progress were approaching, and so one team member, Adam Williams, stepped up to the task of organizing the members to engage in exploration, saying that the team had to divide and conquer and had to get some things done. He decided that someone would have to interview customers about their interests, someone else was needed to look at research, and someone else had to explore technology and compliance issues. Others at Merrill Lynch needed to be contacted so that team members could find interest, support, and ideas inside the company itself. With the tasks organized and spread out before them, team members volunteered for the things they wanted to do. Teammate Tara Shav declared that she had connections in technology and was also close to someone in compliance, so she could investigate whether the team's ideas were even feasible. Kristin Hill took on the task of organizing everything—from PowerPoint presentations to compiling all the data; she wrote everything down and pulled together many of the ideas. Thomas Roszko was to gather information at Merrill Lynch's New York headquarters.

Soon the team's queries brought in lots of ideas. The energy in the team heightened as members noted that people liked to talk to them and provide great ideas about what the product should be. Thomas Roszko (Tom) found pay dirt when he started talking to a senior desk analyst, Raj Sinha. The two brainstormed a number of ideas, but the one that seemed to stick was this notion of trading distressed equities—that is, trading stocks of companies that were coming out of bankruptcy. But they pushed beyond just having their own side of Merrill Lynch—equity—involved. Top management had been stressing the importance of having the debt and equity groups work together more. Raj and Tom believed that the debt side could also be involved in some way and that the company could make money in that arena. Tom knew that this was a real opportunity—it was something new where Merrill Lynch had competitive advantage, an answer to one of top management's needs, and something that the team would have real interest and energy to pursue. And it presented the possibility of financial gain.

But this was only one of three ideas that the team was considering. Members had to spend some time evaluating all three and trying to decide which was best. The rest of the team agreed that Tom and Raj's idea was the best they had; now exploration took a more focused turn to learn more about this one particular idea of trading distressed equities by involving both debt and equity. The Merrill Lynch team was already ahead of the ProPrint team mentioned earlier in the chapter. Its members were able to collect lots of ideas but also to figure out a way to winnow those ideas down and move ahead. The key for flexible phases is to keep the process moving by shifting gears as needed.

So Tom started talking to other people around the company about the idea and "the whole thing just blossomed," he told us later. "If you start talking to people who have more experience than you do, then they ask, 'What about this and what about that? And maybe you should think about this'—and all of a sudden it just took on a life of its own."[6] Tom then enlisted the support of Jeff Campbell and Adam Williams, and the three of them really started to push the idea forward. Tom had come up with a list of twenty-five people to contact who might have some expertise in distressed equity trading, and team members were talking to all of them. Jeff had already worked with MCI and knew how difficult working in distressed equity trading would be. But he saw the potential for change that technology could offer and he worked this angle. And as team members' enthusiasm and expertise started to rise, they garnered some sponsorship from top management. What really gave them the push over the edge, however, was talking to the debt guys.

Since the team members were all on the equities side, they had been talking to people in this part of Merrill Lynch's business. But a key part of exploration and sensemaking is going outside your comfort zone and talking to people who have very different perspectives. So team members ventured to another silo and found someone to talk to on the debt side. They discovered that Merrill Lynch had a large set of analysts: the new product didn't have to be just about trading the companies that were coming out of bankruptcy; the company could use existing expertise in analysis to pick which ones would do better. This work with debt convinced team members that they should create a new joint debt-equity trading desk—a set of people working on the trading floor whose job it is to match buyers and sellers for one particular product or market—that combined sales with analysis and traded distressed equities. Now the idea had evolved from the debt department's offering advice to the traders to actually having debt and equity working together at the same desk.

In the meantime, Tara had been working the compliance side to make sure that the desk that the team was proposing would meet Merrill Lynch's legal and regulatory standards. Things were looking good on that front as well, so everyone was feeling positive about the project.

As the Merrill Lynch example demonstrates so well, the goal of exploration is to collect lots of information and multiple perspectives on what exists now and what is possible going forward. Basically, this first phase is sensemaking. Not coincidentally and as we've already pointed out, this is a primary task of leadership as well. In this phase team members must make sense of their environment and the issue that they are addressing. Included here is understanding the national context, the corporate context, and the multiple interpretations of what the team's task really is. Team members also must hone their understanding of the industry, the market, the technology, the competition, and the customer. They need to comprehend the strategic direction of the firm and the political and cultural environment in which the team must operate.

Sensemaking during exploration involves huge amounts of scouting activity. Scouting becomes a learning activity, with team members trying to comprehend all they can about the terrain that surrounds them. So members need to brainstorm ideas with others around the company. They need to talk to customers to discover needs that are not being met, to look at the competition to see what their own company is missing, and to interview other employees to understand where the pain is. Teams need to explore themselves to find out what would make their lives better and to find out how that meshes with top management's goals. Team members need to talk to other organizational members to find cultural and political traps that threaten the feasibility of their ideas. Finally, they need to talk to people who have tried to solve this problem before so that they do not repeat the same mistakes.

But for scouting to be effective, team members must adopt a mindset that's particular to sensemaking.[7] During the exploration phase, team members need to be able to set aside their preexisting mind-sets and models of the world. They need to be able to put a brake on stereotyping (e.g., "those 'bad' marketing people") and open their minds to taking in new realities and shifts in the landscape that they thought they knew so well. To be an explorer is to look at the world as if it is a new land never seen before.

This new understanding enables the team to achieve another goal of exploration and sensemaking: to create a map, an image, or a story that all team members can share. This map needs to capture key aspects of the external context, the major issue that the team is addressing, and the hoped-for outcomes. This map of the world enables the team to take more informed action, especially if members are able to boil down the complexity of their environment into key patterns and trends. By sharing a map of what's out there as well as what they want to achieve, it is easier to clear a path forward. To the extent that they have seen new and different things and been exposed to great ideas, team members can also be inspired. The Merrill Lynch team was able to move beyond its own domain and see a new possibility—a trading desk that effectively, and structurally, bridged debt and equity and created new value.

From an internal team perspective, the map functions as a source of security. Facing an unknown terrain is scary, pushing the team to turn inward and away from what it does not understand. But the map moves the unknown to the known and enables action. Merrill Lynch team members were able to plot their course forward by mapping the kind of product they wanted to produce and determining the steps required to define what that product would be.

But exploration is not solely the realm of sensemaking, scouting, and map making. Exploration also involves the leadership task of *relating*—that is, establishing relationships with key individuals inside and outside the organization. Of course, one of the primary relationships is with top management, and so a large amount of ambassadorial activity is aimed at representing the team's interests and ideas, lobbying for resources, and linking the team's work to the firm's strategic direction. But this is also the time to get input and buy-in from top management so that they feel some ownership of the team's ideas and become sponsors of the team's activity in the broader political arena of the organization. Top management also may have lots of ideas of how to link the team's ideas to organizational initiatives and to provide a broader perspective of the problems that it faces. Top management, for example, pushed the Merrill Lynch team to go beyond its comfort zone in equities and to explore the new terrain of debt.

In-depth exploration requires large amounts of work inside the team. Extreme execution is needed to create norms of working together and mechanisms to figure out who knows what and how work can best be allocated to members. Team members need to acquire large amounts of information, and that information must be combined and sorted to create a map of the situation. Modes of brainstorming, decision making, and problem solving need to be established.

By the end of a successful exploration phase, there is a set of people committed to the team, patterns of interaction within the team have been developed, and the product or project that the team is working on has been investigated and defined. Hopefully, team members have discovered that the team's goals are feasible and that they can work together to meet those goals. If the team has done its external work well, then this phase also results in a set of external relationships that can help it adapt to its environment and get the information, expertise, and support it needs. Then the major challenge becomes moving from the world of ideas and possibilities into the world of reality and focus. Not every team makes it.

Unlike the ProPrint team, Merrill Lynch team members did make the leap, completing the exploration phase of the project. They had covered a lot of ground, interviewing many people inside and customers outside the company. They had considered many alternatives and after some comparison had settled on one. They had developed and pushed an idea that met top management's strategy of having debt and equity work more closely together, and they had found a project that they thought could win in the marketplace. Their distressed equity desk built on existing expertise within Merrill Lynch and was supported by many individuals throughout the firm. Now the questions to ask were: Could they move from idea to reality? And what would that reality look like?

## Exploitation

Unlike exploration, during which a team spends considerable energy determining what's out there, exploitation is about choosing one option and making it happen. This is when the team transforms its abstract ideas into a reality. In this stage team members face the dilemma of focusing internally on the real work of creating a concrete product that meets expectations while still maintaining and building relationships with outside groups. The team still needs the support and blessing from upper-level managers, still needs external information and expertise, and now needs to work even more closely with other teams with whom coordination is essential.

Although exploration has a heavy focus on sensemaking and relating, which requires lots of scouting and ambassadorial activity, exploitation focuses on *visioning* and *inventing*. Exploitation requires that team members decide what they really want to do and how they will organize themselves to move toward their vision. The shift here is from seeking lots of information and viewpoints and seeing the world with new eyes to choosing one direction and figuring out the best way to make it a reality. The shift is from divergent thinking in multiple directions to convergence and commitment to one.[8]

Once a new direction has been chosen, team members need to produce a prototype of the product or process they are trying to create or to enact a plan for how they will sell a product or consult to a region. What specific features and form will the team's product have? What options are most important, and what trade-offs will have to be made?

In the exploitation phase, scouting, ambassadorial activity, and task coordination are of a very different nature than they were during exploration.

Scouting is about looking at how other teams have implemented similar efforts and searching for best practices. Scouting may also be about getting potential customers' reactions to the team's ideas. But compared to the exploration phase, scouting activity decreases during exploitation. Ambassadorship is about keeping upper-level managers informed, keeping up their interest, and getting their ideas about how to move into specifics. Again, the level of this external activity decreases, since buy-in has been established and now only needs to be maintained. Task coordination, however, takes on a much larger role as the team finds other groups whose input will be essential for bringing the new idea into the light of day. These groups need to be linked to the team's schedule and sometimes cajoled into helping.

A clear dilemma at the exploitation phase is how much to separate the team from the rest of the organization. Isolation enables the team to work in a more focused manner on the prototype, without as many interruptions and interference from the myriad people who have a stake in the team's outcomes. The team is able to make its transition without outsiders constantly telling the team to add this or think about that. The greater the isolation, however, the greater the probability that the team will develop a shell around itself. This shell can become a barrier between "us" and "them," making outsiders feel like enemies instead of friends and making the shift to exportation that much more difficult later on. The Merrill Lynch team chose to stay very connected to the rest of the organization during this time.

The Merrill Lynch team members knew that they were at a transition point. They spent time discussing their vision to have a distressed equities desk that spanned debt and equity—something that had never been done before. They knew they had a great idea, but now they had to figure out how it could actually be done. They moved to the specifics of estimating how the desk would work, who would have to be involved, and how much money they thought they could make. They decided to put a plan in place so that their project could be a reality in three to six months if the team received the go-ahead.

This move to making the product a reality meant a lot of work in the systems area. Tara was trying to figure out how the desk would actually work, considering questions like these: Does the salesperson in the high-yield desk send the trader an order? And what does the order management system look like? And how—and in what form—do you get your market data? Tara was working with three or four different people in systems to work some of this out. There was scouting work to determine what the systems people would need to know to make the desk work and a lot of task coordination to figure out how the team would actually work with the systems people.

Meanwhile, Adam and Kristin were doing a lot of the organizing—putting the team's work down on paper, making sure people were making the calls that needed to be made, making sure that assignments were done and handed in on time. Tom, Jeff, and Adam were also still doing a lot of the networking, trying to test the team's ideas and getting projections on how much money could be made. With additional ambassadorial activity, they figured that this would be an important part of management's decision to move ahead or not.

There were a lot of details to be worked out because trading distressed equities is complicated. One week there might be a hundred companies coming out of bankruptcy, and another week there might be only one. Jeff took on a lot of the work here, deciding to do a case study. He basically said, "All right, let's look at four names that have recently come out of bankruptcy. What kinds of volumes did they trade? If Merrill Lynch went in with this new desk, how many shares would we have traded, and how much would we have made?" Team members went through a variety of scenarios of what might have happened with different interventions. Then they worked through staffing: How many people would be needed, and how much would they have to be paid? And where would the desk be, in debt or equity? So a big part of the exploitation phase for the Merrill Lynch team was running scenarios and creating prototypes to fit the kinds of situations that the desk might face. After examining the effectiveness of multiple prototypes in a variety of scenarios, the choice about what to actually do, or make, becomes easier and more efficient.

Meanwhile, Tom was busy "picking the brains" of two of his colleagues who ran similar desks. They had done comparable kinds of analyses, and so Tom decided to learn as much from them as possible. Thus, scouting continues throughout this process, but there is a lot of time spent figuring out how others have done similar things and then trying to improve on and adapt those practices. In exploitation the scouting is not about discovering a new way to see the surrounding terrain but about getting information and expertise on the proposed solution.

And so the Merrill Lynch team worked its way through exploitation— and its product idea moved from concept to reality. Team members were clear and committed to the vision of what they wanted to create, and they had to invent the structures and processes to get them there. This phase might also be called "execution"—that is, getting the job done. The team continued its scouting and vicarious learning, but now it was focused on the details of how this desk would actually work. The team continued to garner support and engage in ambassadorial activity—but not as much as in the exploration phase. And now the team members were more focused on task coordination—getting ideas and feedback about the functioning of the desk and coordinating with the systems and compliance people who had to design the systems and approve the activities that would take place at the new desk. Internal team meetings focused on brainstorming the best design that members could put together.

The team was able to move from idea to reality. Now it was time to see whether it could spread that enthusiasm and expertise to others and test-market its new product to get feedback and do further refinements.

## Exportation

Like most teams, the Merrill Lynch team wanted its project to get implemented. Members were given two chances to make presentations to top management, and they were determined to make their case. They continued their scouting, now aimed at understanding how best to present and convince the top brass that their ideas should be chosen. They continued their ambassadorship by getting the support of as many managers as they could. They wanted commitments that these managers would work with the new desk if it was created. They continued to do task coordination, trying their ideas out on other groups and creating new ways that the desk could operate. And they continued to work as a highly honed team with members working hard in what were now their established roles.

Kristin was putting together presentations and PowerPoint slides and setting up all the logistics. Other members chipped in suggestions. They thought long and hard about how to best present their ideas. How could they best capture top management's attention? Jeff would be the one to focus on the case study since he was the one who had the actual experience trading some of the key stocks, while Adam was more adept at looking at the overall picture. Tara had the systems and compliance issues covered, and Tom had the details of the core idea. The team had definitely united together around their proposal. Now they wanted everyone else to know what a great idea they had.

There were several other team presentations to Dow Kim, the executive vice president and president of global markets and investment banking, on the day that the Merrill Lynch team members made theirs. Team members were very nervous but determined to show that they could really make a difference. The presentation went well, and they got some very positive feedback from Dow. It was a very happy team that left the conference room that evening to head out to dinner. Later team members learned that Dow had decided to move ahead, and the new desk was created. A senior manager, Corey Carlesimo, who had been involved with the project from the beginning, officially started the desk, but team members continued to provide background, advice, and guidance to him. They had been noticed for their innovative work, and that exposure continued as they helped the new distressed equity team fine-tune their design and market the new desk.

As the Merrill Lynch team illustrates, exportation involves taking what the team has done and moving it out into the organization and perhaps the marketplace. Here team members need to transfer their knowledge and enthusiasm to others who will continue their work. Exportation might mean moving from a prototype to large-scale manufacturing and marketing, or it might mean taking a tool that worked very well in one department and implementing it in other ones. In exportation team members are challenged to effectively communicate all the tacit knowledge they have to others and to motivate others to take on something that those people might not understand or want to do. Team members also have to figure out the best way to present the work that they have done; they often focus too much on details and not enough on why others should care at all.

This is another transition for the team, and it is often a tough one. Sometimes team members cannot let go. They feel that the product or process they have created is never quite right and they need to keep working on it. Sometimes team members feel as if no one else in the organization will really understand and appreciate the work that they have done, and so they are hesitant to share their knowledge with others. In addition, the isolation that facilitates effective exploitation can hamper the team members' ability to export. But even if the team is OK with the transition, sometimes there is no one waiting at the other end. Whatever problem moving from exploitation to exportation presents, without this transfer of enthusiasm and ownership, team members may find their work rejected or simply left to wither and die.

This chapter has outlined three phases of team activity: exploration, exploitation, and exportation. These phases are similar to the ones that were described by the CEO of IDEO, Tim Brown, when he was speaking at the MIT Sloan School of Management in 2006. IDEO, a Palo Alto–based product design firm famous for its innovation, asks its team members during the first phase of product development to act like anthropologists trying to understand how a product is used and understood by all the key stakeholders. For example, when designing a new emergency room layout, IDEO employees attached a camera to the head of a patient. After watching ten hours of pictures of the ceiling, the patient perspective was clear. And it was one the hospital staff did not fully realize. This process is exactly what we mean by exploration.

Then, in the second phase at IDEO, team members brainstorm multiple possible designs and engage in rapid prototyping to test different solutions and determine which work best. They then move to choosing one design through a multivoter process—a step similar to exploitation. Finally, the team demonstrates its product to top management within IDEO and within the client company. Members also field-test the product with potential customers. This stage is similar to exportation.

Each of the three phases of activity—exploration, exploitation, and exportation—also demonstrates a different sequence of leadership capabilities. Flexible phases become the vehicle through which the X-team demonstrates distributed leadership in action. It is the X-team that moves the team through sensemaking and relating, then visioning and inventing, then relating again. It is the X-team that distributes these key leadership capabilities to team members, management, customers, experts, and other organizational members as members engage in external activity shifts across phases. It is the X-team that actually puts breath and detail into visions and strategies from on high as it becomes the eyes of the organization, produces the products, enacts the processes, and spreads the practices that become the real output of the organization. It is the

X-team that translates big ideas into concrete projects and action, which, in turn, shape the firm's future strategies.

In this chapter, we've shown the three phases of exploration, exploitation, and exportation as following one another sequentially and as three clearly separate modes of activity. In reality, the process is not always so neat. As another team at Merrill Lynch illustrates, the road is not always so smooth. This other team was well into exploitation only to discover that Merrill Lynch's lawyers found the product too risky and would not give their approval to move ahead. The team, therefore, had to move back into exploration mode and return to one of the earlier options on the table. Another team learned that an idea the members were trying to implement had been tried before and that one set of customers had been very resistant. This team went back to exploitation and tried to make some changes to the product that would appeal to this customer base. Even so, despite the twists and turns of these teams, members often find that using the road map of exploration, exploitation, and exportation helps them stay focused and shift gears as needed.

At the time of this writing, the Merrill Lynch team's desk has been trading distressed equities for about two years. The first year was a learning and building phase and generated millions of dollars in revenue. The second year the desk was restructured to achieve a better allocation of people and tools and to broaden the desk's responsibilities. The desk increased from two people to six, and the number of companies covered doubled. Daily trading volume is up about fifteenfold, and revenue is on pace to generate twenty times that of the first year. Clearly, trading distressed equities has proved to be a valuable business, and Merrill Lynch has enjoyed first-mover advantage.

Thus, through exploration, exploitation, and exportation, the Merrill Lynch team fulfilled its members' goals and made a difference in their personal learning, their careers, and their contribution to the company. From a competitive standpoint Merrill Lynch gained a new product that contributed to the bottom line and that was ahead of its competitors. And from a distributed leadership perspective, the team had brought together top management and traders, people from debt and people from equity, customers and lawyers, and a host of others who together achieved the corporate goal of joining debt and equity and giving it a face. Team members distributed the tasks of sensemaking, relating, inventing, and visioning to multiple individuals as they moved across phases.

Now the questions to ask are: How does one enable this flexibility, agility, and distributed leadership? What structures can be put in place to support X-teams in action? The answers are the focus of our next chapter.

# SIX

# X-Factors

## *The X-Team Support Structure*

HILLARY CLINTON once argued that it "takes a village" to raise a child.[1] Here we suggest that it takes an X-team to engage in distributed leadership through its ability to innovate, adapt, and bring life to corporate strategies. But the X-team is not a simple solution: it requires melding internal and external activities, shifting activities over time, and linking the passion and voice from below to the big picture on high and to the expertise distributed all around. Given such complexity, how is it possible to structure a team to make all of this happen? The answer lies in what we call the three "X-factors," which are the core design features of an X-team: extensive ties, expandable tiers, and exchangeable membership.

If the three X-team principles that we've looked at so far are the processes that drive X-team success, then X-factors form the underlying structure that supports these processes (see figure 6-1). *Extensive ties* link the team to the intricate network involving different kinds of relationships to myriad people in multiple locations. *Expandable tiers* enable team members to work together effectively while creating the flexibility needed to shift activity across tasks and in response to a changing environment. The tiers work to differentiate among different roles and levels of commitment in the team. Lastly, *exchangeable membership* allows the people who compose the team to shift over time so that the appropriate mix of skills and abilities is available when needed.

Let's look at the story of how the Netgen team at Microsoft relied on the X-factors as it moved through exploration, exploitation, and exportation. A team that was extraordinarily creative in its approach to product development, Netgen succeeded despite numerous setbacks and

**FIGURE 6-1**

## X-factors

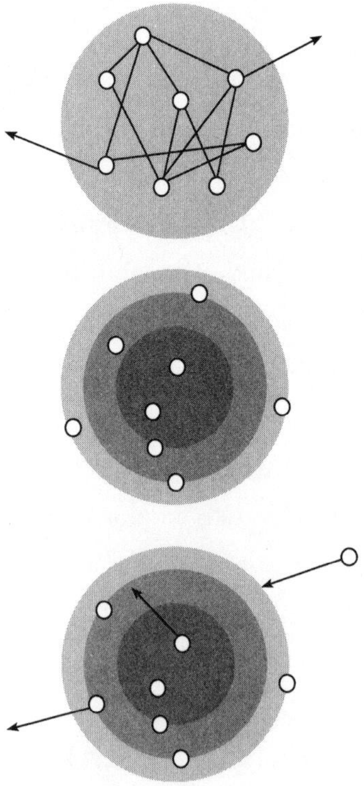

**Extensive ties**

- Know who to contact
- Make use of weak ties
- Make use of strong ties

**Expandable tiers**

- **Core:** creates team strategy and makes key decisions, coordinates other parts of team, carries history and identity of team
- **Operational:** carries out ongoing work of team
- **Outer net:** specialized or separable task, part-time or part-cycle members

**Exchangeable membership**

- People shift in and out of team
- People shift across tiers
- Different tiers have different membership expectations

lack of support. Not only did it create a new software product for the Internet generation; it also pushed the limits on how Microsoft incorporates customers into the product development process.

## In the Beginning: Exploration

After twelve years at Microsoft, Tammy Savage found herself working in a business strategy role trying to figure out what the company should build in the future. She and her team, Michael Furdyk and Jennifer Corriero, soon began to focus on one particular customer group, the "Net generation"—people, age thirteen to twenty-four, who had grown up on the Internet. These "Netgeners" were mouse trained before they were toilet trained. Tammy believed that they used technology in a very different way than other generations because they integrated technology in their daily life. She also believed that Microsoft did not fully understand this new customer group.

To explore this idea Tammy spent a few hours talking to an author, Don Tapscott, who studied Netgeners. Although she became convinced that Netgeners' capacity to do things with technology was different from other customer groups, she didn't know what, specifically, was different about them. She decided to put together a team of "anthropologists" who joined Tammy, Michael, and Jennifer to observe and study Netgeners' use of technology.

When a friend of Tammy's mentioned that her alma mater had a monthlong break coming up and that students were looking for projects, Tammy jumped at the opportunity. She put together a project whereby a dozen college students lived in a house for three weeks and worked together to develop a business plan. Tammy and a small team from Microsoft watched them around the clock. The team was not interested in the plan itself, but rather in how the college students related to technology while putting the plan together. Team members learned multiple things. While the college students said that the Internet was not that important to them, in reality it was something they effortlessly and continually relied upon. "It was like oxygen to them," Tammy suggested.[2] These students lived on the Internet, logging on before they had coffee in the morning and hopping on and off until late at night. They were instant-messaging their friends, looking things up, or buying clothes. They took the Internet for granted, using it at every turn as a way to get through daily life.

From these observations Tammy created a story that brought the situation to life. Basically, she compared and contrasted this Net generation with the "PC generation" and the "TV generation." At this point Michael and Jennifer had run out of assignments, and two-thirds of the team was transferred to another manager. Tammy and the others went around Microsoft and started introducing people to the Netgeners. Tammy became a crusader to push the company to figure out how to serve these new, young technology adopters before someone else stole them away. She shared the Netgen story with people in every Microsoft division. "One meeting would result in three more. One person would hear the story, and then they wanted the entire team to hear it . . . until thousands of people had heard it from the bottom to the top of the organization," she explained.

This process resulted in many supporters and a few skeptics. On the support side were Nadine Yount, who introduced Tammy to Linda Stone and J Allard. Linda became a mentor, and J and Nadine contributed to the team dialogue. Tammy met Jim Allchin, who would later fund the project and introduce her to a member of Microsoft's board of directors. At the same time Tammy and her team received a boost from outside the company as publications like *Fortune* wrote stories about the project.[3]

One of the skeptics was Bill Gates. Bill didn't want to just learn that certain customers were different; he wanted to know how existing products should change and which new ones should be built based on those differences. Tammy didn't have any of these answers. She was educating people and leaving it up to product development to decide what to do. However, when the challenge came, Tammy determined that it was time to confront these questions.

Tammy decided that whatever did get built would have to be in the Internet services group (ISG). The president of the ISG, Rick Belluzzo, agreed to fund the project, but after three months there was still no funding. Then David Cole, also in the ISG, agreed to fund a small team and incubate the project.

While all of this political maneuvering was going on to get resources and keep the project alive, Tammy was introduced to Melora Zaner who had been studying teenage girls—part of the Netgen population. Melora's research suggested that teens like to share experiences and emotions and to gossip. Or a teen might be listening to music and want her friends to hear it too. For teens, Melora believed, technology could be used to enhance their need to express emotion, build an identity, and maintain relationships. So when Tammy started to work with Melora, the project's focus changed from technology aimed at improving productivity to technology that touched people at a social level. Melora became the project manager, and the two started to build the rest of the Netgen X-team.

The next step was to hire a bunch of college students and start figuring out what kind of software they might actually develop for Netgeners. Soon there were some developers and designers on board, and the team grew to nine (C.J., Kate, Erica, Bubba, Rama, Ezar, and Eugene joined Tammy and Melora). They moved the team from Microsoft headquarters in Redmond, Washington, to the more urban Seattle, where they set up shop in a space with an open floor plan so that ideas could flow. The new team members were smart, creative people who had grown up on the Internet and used it a lot. They wanted to see how they could stretch its technological boundaries.

They were going to produce something new and exciting for their customers—and they were the customer. They wanted to create a product that would affect people's lives in a meaningful way and that would go beyond one-on-one interaction, making it possible to do things on the Internet as a group.

In the summer of 2000, the new team went on a three-day retreat to get to know each other and learn about the research that Tammy and Melora had already done. They did massive amounts of brainstorming, sometimes using their own experiences to confirm some ideas from the early research, reject others, and push some even further. Following the retreat, these new college recruits had to learn how to get up in front of Microsoft executives and pitch the team's ideas in what was known as the "target"—or vision of what Netgeners wanted and how the team would meet those needs. As Kathleen Mulcahy (Kate) described, team members explained that Netgeners care about friends, fun, and music, with an emphasis on socializing and developing an identity—not just about work productivity.[4]

For these college graduates, joining the team was a peak experience. They were building something new and different—creating a revolution at Microsoft. And they got instant exposure to senior managers, including Bill Gates, as they went around the company presenting the target. But then the ISG began to scale back incubation efforts, and David Cole had to cancel the project. Now new funding had to be found. Some team members left, and the others were unsure what the future would hold. But the passion was there, and the sense was that they had to continue. What had begun as Tammy Savage's idea had clearly and quickly become the domain of the whole team.

Despite numerous setbacks, team members had been very successful at exploration. From early on there was a high level of scouting to learn as much as possible about this new customer, with Tammy talking to the author of a book on the Internet generation and Melora scouring the research on how Netgeners developed, as well as on their social, psychological, and emotional lives. Other members of the team conducted numerous interviews and focus group sessions with Netgeners to understand their reactions to the products the team was creating, as well as what was important to them in life and technology. Team members spent time trying to understand what other products existed in this domain, inside and outside Microsoft. They also learned from their own responses to new product ideas. By the end of this exploration phase, they had done a great deal of sensemaking and came to have a new and deep understanding of the customer, the market, and the technology.

While task coordination would become instrumental later in the process, this external activity was less pronounced during the exploration phase. Ambassadorial activity, by contrast, was evident from the start. As soon as Tammy saw that the Netgeners were different and presented a real business opportunity, she became a crusader. She worked on getting buy-in and support—going right to the top of the organization and continuing down several levels. But Tammy was not in this alone. The newly hired Netgen team all learned the target and delivered it to top-level managers, thus creating a whole team of ambassadors. Tammy often brought other team members with her when she had meetings with top managers to get the next round of funding. This forced these team members to put themselves in top management's shoes and answer this question: why would the company want to produce such a product? Thus, exploration involved relating with multiple stakeholders and getting a sense of organizational priorities. It created distributed leadership in action as people below top management moved to innovate, change corporate culture, and bring a new product to life because they passionately believed in a new vision for product development that started with the customer. All of this success was facilitated by the three X-factors.

### Extensive Ties

To engage in the kind of external activity just described, team members need extensive ties with outsiders. *Weak ties*, those relationships with people we do not know very well, help teams round up handy knowledge and expertise inside or outside the company. Here members can easily call on people because they are not asking for very much. *Strong ties*, on the other hand, facilitate higher levels of cooperation and the transfer of complex knowledge. These ties are most likely forged when relationships are critical to both sides and build over long periods. Strong ties help when a team member is asking for significant resources or help.[5]

Both types of ties, weak and strong, help team members feel as if they have the capability of reaching out across their boundaries to seek the input they need from outside. Much time can be lost if no such ties exist and the team does not know where to find critical expertise, resources, and support.

The Netgen team made use of many ties to accomplish its work. From the very beginning Tammy used her extensive contacts to help move the team along. A weak tie to a college grad she knew resulted in her gaining access to a group of students in need of a project during a school break. Tammy's extensive ties to top management enabled her to get the resources that she needed, to spread the word about Netgeners, and to stave off the multiple individuals who wanted to kill the project. Some of these ties to top management were quite strong, built up over multiple years, and diligently maintained. When Tammy needed to influence a senior manager, she sometimes did it herself, but at other times she worked with a senior manager whom she already knew to have more impact.

In fact, it was one such tie that led to Tammy's introduction to Melora. In turn, Melora brought her extensive ties to researchers. Melora's expertise, critical to the development of the product, was fueled by access to a research and programming network inside Microsoft and a university community outside.

The use of ties became a central norm of the Netgen team. The new recruits brought ties to their friends and their universities. These ties enabled the team to easily test and retest its ideas on many campuses and to connect to other potential customers. When the team faced a problem for which it had no existing ties to help with the solution, it was not shy but acted quickly to create new ties to gain the support, expertise, and commitment needed for exploration. Without this infrastructure of ties, scouting, ambassadorship, and task coordination are exponentially more difficult.

### Expandable Tiers

But how do you structure a team that has a strong identity and solid psychological safety while simultaneously maintaining dense ties and doing the necessary external activity to get the job done? The answer is by employing expandable tiers within the team. X-teams operate through three distinct tiers that create differentiated types of team membership—the core, operational layer, and outer-net tier—with members performing duties within more than one tier.

*The core membership.* The core of the X-team is often, but not always, present at the start of the team. Core members carry the team's history and identity. They are often the first to have the vision and passion that carry the team through tough times—as such, the core often contains the team's leaders. While simultaneously coordinating the multiple parts of the team, the core members create the team strategy and make key decisions. They understand why early decisions were made and can offer a rationale for current decisions and structures. The core is not a management level, however. Core members frequently work beside other members of equal or higher rank and serve on other X-teams as operational or outer-net members.

At first, Tammy, Michael, and Jennifer were the only core members of the team. They communicated the team's values and vision and worked to create the structure and resources needed to show that the Netgen product was essential for Microsoft. Later, when those early team members left, the core extended to Melora, who became another crusader for the product. Melora also worked to create a bigger team and to manage the different tiers.

As a team evolves, more people often join the core. Having multiple people in the core helps keep the team going when one or two core members leave, and it allows a core member who gets very involved with operational work to hand off core tasks. This is one mode of distributing leadership across multiple individuals who share core leadership responsibilities. Teams that lose all their core members at once take many months to get back on track.

*Operational members.* The team's operational members do the ongoing work. Whether that's designing a computer or deciding where to drill for oil, the operational members get the job done. They often are tightly connected to one another and to the core. There may be a wide range of operational members handling different aspects of the X-team task. The key for these team members is to focus on what they have to do and how best to do it. They handle the coordination needed to get their own job done, but they leave full team coordination to the core members. Similarly, operational members seem to be more motivated if they share the vision and values of the team and understand the importance of what the team is working toward. They are usually not the creators of that vision (unless they are also core members) but often have a large impact on shaping the evolution of the team over time.

The Netgen team had several different sets of operational members. Early on there was the team of anthropologists, whose task it was to monitor the activities of the college students to try to understand how the Net generation perceived and used technology. Later, this set of folks went on to other work, and a different set of operational members emerged to carry out the tasks of brainstorming and understanding the customer, markets, and technologies. Operational membership changes as the skills and abilities needed to get the work done shift.

*Outer-net members.* Outer-net members often join the team to handle some task that is separable from ongoing work. They may be part-time or part-cycle members, tied barely at all to one another but strongly to the operational or core members.[6] Outer-net members bring specialized expertise, and different individuals may participate in the outer net as the task of the team changes. Outer-net members often do not feel as committed to the team or its product because they are not necessarily in the team for long, they are often physically separated from other members, and they do not necessarily participate in integrative meetings or social events. Furthermore, they may report to a different part of the organization.

Early on the Netgen team did not have many outer-net members. The author of the Internet book and the college students who worked on the business plan became a bit like outer-net members when they offered their insights on how Netgeners work and feel about technology. Also, Nadine Yount, Linda Stone, and J. Allard became mentors to Tammy while reporters from *Fortune* and other similar publications became short-term PR for the whole team.

A similar three-tier structure is currently in use at a small entrepreneurial start-up we know—except that the employees there say "pigs," "chickens," and "cows" to refer to core, operational, and outer-net team members. Think about a bacon-and-egg breakfast: the pig is very committed, the chicken is involved, and the cow provides milk that enhances the meal. The start-up's terminology is handy for discussing roles and responsibilities. A person might say, "You don't need to worry about that; you're only a chicken" or "We need this cow to graze here for at least two weeks."

### Exchangeable Membership

Our third X-factor, exchangeable membership, refers to the fact that X-team membership is fluid. People move in and out of the team during its life or move between tiers. In fact, one of the hallmarks of an X-team is its ability to adapt to changes in the team's task and environment. Even the movement from exploration to exploitation and exportation involves a shift from discovery to development to diffusion—three very dissimilar tasks. To facilitate this adaptation and shift from one task to another, from one set of external conditions to another, from one mode of operation to another, exchanging members is necessary. Seldom is one set of people configured in one way able to make the necessary changes over a team's lifetime. Even if they were capable of doing so, many members of X-teams move on to do something else, thereby requiring that the X-team membership changes.

The Netgen team followed a common pattern: one person or a small group of people engaged at the beginning, followed by growth and change of team membership, and then a gradual decrease in membership toward the end. The Netgen team, like many others, also shifted its core, operational, and outer-net membership as the task changed and the need for different skills, ties, and areas of expertise morphed.

In examining the history of the Netgen team, a number of membership changes are clear. First, Tammy, Michael, and Jennifer as core were joined by the anthropologists to do a specific piece of work. Then most of these people moved on. Next, Melora came on board, thus shifting the focus of the core task. This core group then added a number of operational members who were new to the organization and who brought in fresh ideas and contacts with many other Netgeners. The team was set up for exploration. At this stage Tammy and Melora were the core members organizing the team, but they were also very much operational members participating in the brainstorming and inquiry that typifies this phase.

The Netgen team had successfully navigated exploration, investigating the needs of the Internet generation. Now it was time to stop thinking about all the things that the software could do and figure out a way to keep the team alive so members could focus on the features that they really wanted to design, develop, and test. The three X-factors enabled this shift to exploitation.

## Making the Dream into Reality: Exploitation

One thing was clear: team members were not willing to give up. Tammy went to Jim Allchin, a member of the top management team, and asked him to fund the project. He agreed and sent her to work under Will Poole. Will gave her the go-ahead to put together a team to actually build the product.

The team restarted with a high level of uncertainty. Would Tammy continue to lead the effort though she had never built a product? The answer was yes: Will Poole was willing to take a risk. Would the team be able to work in their urban environment (Seattle) or have to move back to company headquarters (Redmond, Washington). After some convincing, the team was allowed to stay in their big, open space in Seattle. Would the team be able to build the technology and get it out the door while dealing with the political shifts that resulted in threats to funding? Yes, but the team needed to use ties, tiers, and exchangeable membership to meet these challenges.

All the brainstorming and inquiry done during exploration finally came together in the team's first prototype, code-named Vogue. But, of course, members did not get this first pass at Vogue completely right, so they were constantly meeting with customers and conducting focus groups. They would create prototypes of new features, get feedback from customers, make changes, go to top management and ask for more funding, and then do the same thing all over again. Throughout this period team members reported spurts of activity around "fire drills": first came an executive review and dates by which code would have to be written, and then everyone worked like maniacs to make their deadlines. As one team member reported, "We definitely learned to kick butt." But, still, the critics wondered whether the team would ever ship anything.

In December 2001, Tammy hired John Vert, a development manager. With his ten years at Microsoft and extensive experience in shipping products, John brought new expertise to the team. At this point some of the early team members left, while others, including C.J. and Kate, stayed on board. John's expertise also helped convince Jim Allchin that the product would see the light of day, so Jim made sure the team's funding continued.

John gave the team a bit of a reality check by showing members exactly what it takes to ship a product. After reflecting on John's advice, the team decided to trim down the Vogue prototype, get this simplified version out to the people in beta testing, find out what customers thought, use the feedback to make changes, and then ship. By limiting the scope of the product, software development would be able to move much faster, customers would not be overwhelmed, and additional features could be added later. Kate and others took the simplified prototype on the road and got lots of feedback, and by February 2002, the team had a plan for the Netgen software.

To make this transition to product design happen, the team structure was more defined, with program managers who each owned a specific set of features. For example, C.J. owned MusicMix because he was a true aficionado who wanted to see to it that music could be shared between groups. He was the one who was most passionate about the feature, and he had a very good idea of the technology that would get it all to work. Kate was Winks, which enabled people to send emotions and animations, like a hug.

Now team members started to write the complete specs, which brought them into contact with a lot of other Microsoft teams because they did not want to recreate technology that already existed. The team was working with engineers to get new technologies built that it needed to work with Windows' peer-to-peer technology. Some Netgen members started working with a team in Redmond to test pieces of software that they had already created. They also decided to work with the peer networking team (PNT) to figure out how to connect the groups of people who would share music and experiences. An important part of that process, though, meant sending a few Netgen teammates to meet with Todd Manion, a PNT member, to decide how Netgen and PNT would work together. Todd was also a recent college graduate who worked well with the Netgen team and became an evangelist for the product back in PNT.

Working with all of these other groups was exhausting, but then in February 2003, the beta—now called threedegrees (as in three degrees of separation, so that customers would make an association with close connections)—was shipped. The team had a big party, and the shipment garnered the attention of people at Microsoft. Before people thought, "Tammy's got some crazy college kids, and she thinks she's going to change the world." Suddenly, the consensus was, "Oh, wow, that team actually shipped a piece of software for Microsoft." People were impressed. The team had taken a mere idea and created a product that customers could actually use.

Still, the exploitation phase was not over yet. For one thing, the team had to work on an international version. For another, suddenly, they had real live customers to deal with—customers who wanted product support and who provided lots of feedback about the product. Moreover, the marketing and PR people got involved. Tammy rehired Caroline Rocky, who had recruited many of the original Netgen team members, and asked her to consolidate all the data coming in on customer reactions. Tammy and the team started thinking about the next version of the product, code-named Mosquito ("Mosquito" was a tongue-and-cheek response to MSN Butterfly).

To assist with managing and setting priorities for Mosquito, Jonathan Sposato was brought in to be group manager. New program managers were also brought into the team to expand the features of the product. Samir was in charge of the Game Lobby, which would enable people to play games together. Joe was in charge of Flicks, a video-mix program that would allow people to share video clips, and Bubbles, whereby members of a group of friends (or "circle") could send each other gifts like a poem or piece of music. Heather, as the most junior program manager, would have to work on a bit of everything.

But the decision was then made to merge the Netgen team into the Microsoft Messenger team, and its core task shifted to exporting ideas and enthusiasm to those back in the center of Microsoft.

The Netgen team had now successfully navigated through the exploitation phase. Members had created a vision of what kind of product they wanted to build, and they had invented a beta version of the product and sent it to the marketplace. They had engaged in scouting throughout the firm to find pockets of expertise needed to develop the product. Furthermore, they had continued to garner the support of top management and achieve continued funding for their development efforts. Finally, they had coordinated with many different groups throughout Microsoft that were creating different pieces of the software product or helping test the code that had already been produced. Internally, team members had added people who provided needed expertise to the team and continued to work effectively as a group and with customers. From a distributed leadership standpoint, they had brought together dozens of people inside and outside the company to create a new product to meet the needs of a new customer.

### The X-Factors and Exploitation

Again, much of this exploitation activity was made possible by the three X-factors (extensive ties, expandable tiers, and exchangeable membership). In addition to keeping up the ties used during exploration, the Netgen team added more. John Vert was able to help speed the shipping of the first beta product because of his expertise and also because of his many contacts throughout Microsoft. When there was a question, problem, or glitch, John knew whom to call to get answers and smooth the way. Jonathan Sposato was brought on board to do the same thing with Mosquito. The rest of the Netgen team members continued to use their extensive set of ties to their classmates and alma maters to get fast feedback on product features from the college set, and Tammy and Melora leveraged their networks to find the right people for the large task of coordinating with other groups.

While only Tammy and Melora were part of the core during exploration, the core expanded during exploitation. In this second phase C.J., Kate, Eugene, and Erica—all of whom had internalized the core rationale for a Netgen product and were coordinating separate features of the product (e.g., music, Winks, etc.)—became part of the core. This set of people worked both to do their part of the team's project while also contributing to the overall plan of how the pieces would fit together. John Vert also joined the core, and he helped bring greater organization to this new group of core members. Later Jonathan Sposato would join the core with Samir, Joe, and Heather.

More operational members were added during exploitation since more people were needed to create the code for the beta features and then to move on to the next version of the product. These operational members worked closely with the new outer-net members. Included in the latter group were experts in peer-to-peer technology; members of the peer networking team, who took on some of the basic design work to create a peer-to-peer application for the product; and members of a testing group who would make sure that the beta product would be ready to release in the market. When the beta shipped, other outer-net members from marketing and PR joined the team to ensure that threedegrees had a smooth launch. In a sense one could even argue that some of the customers became outer-net members at this point since several were engaged in a heated dialogue with operational members, discussing what they would like to see changed in the product.

Thus, the three-tier structure helps organize an X-team's activities and enable members to understand their roles and responsibilities. Operational members focus on getting the work done while core members also help organize the team and plan the strategy for the whole. The outer-net members get pulled into the team's work and culture as they are needed but remain part of their regular organizational units. The tiers help the team expand and contract in an orderly manner and enable people to come on board quickly, since they recognize the type of commitment they are making. The tiers also offer a way of organizing the work of a fairly large number of people spread throughout and even outside the firm.

Exchangeable membership was also evident in the shift from exploration to exploitation. Perhaps the biggest change was shifting some of the operational members into core member roles, to organize the team and separate parts of the task, and then adding John Vert to organize the core group, and later Jonathan Sposato. Members of the operational team shifted as well. Some favored the excitement, brainstorming, creativity, and low levels of structure of the exploration phase. As the team moved on, those people resisted the increased formalization, breaking the task up into subtasks, the adherence to schedules, and the interdependence that is often part of the exploitation phase. These members left the team. Other team members left for personal reasons (a girlfriend in LA) or because they decided they wanted a different kind of career. But others were more than ready to shepherd the prototype into the land of reality and to continue the testing and refining necessary to have a viable beta product that customers could actually use. These members stayed and others joined their ranks. In addition, many outer-net members were added from other parts of Microsoft to bring technological expertise to the Netgen team. In this phase even Tammy and Melora shifted roles, moving away from operational tasks and more toward securing the resources and support needed from other parts of the organization.

## Integrating Back into Microsoft: Exportation

During exploration and exploitation, the Netgen team had remained quite separated from Microsoft—after all, it was in Seattle rather than in Redmond. But exportation meant joining up with Microsoft Messenger, and the core job became integrating the work of the team within this larger unit in Redmond. The Netgen team members had conceived of a great product through a deep understanding of the customer, fought many political battles to get resources, and then created the software to make their dream a reality. But now their independent work was done, and it was time to leverage that work and export it to the rest of the company. The people in the Messenger group saw the business value of what the team was doing. As Tammy commented in an interview with one of us, "We were like an organ that was being rejected by the body. And the only way that the body was going to accept it was if the donor gave it up and the body was responsible for it." So she and her team members had to allow the Messenger folks to take charge of the product, and letting go was very difficult.

The move into exportation to Messenger brought with it many changes—most significantly, the team split up. Tammy and a few other members actually left the group to create the Customer Design Center and bring the voice of the customer to other products. Bill Gates had come full circle and now believed that the kind of work that Tammy and the Netgen team had done was critical and a best practice in the company. It was the premier example of how Microsoft should take the time to understand the user experience so deeply, making prototypes of what features customers might want, and then getting feedback.

Other team members had to move into Messenger to link the Mosquito features into Messenger's product. Jonathan Sposato stepped into a leadership role in integrating Netgen with Messenger. His first management challenge was to coach Netgeners to "lower your shields, we're all on the same side." Messenger was now funding the Netgen team, and its product was the platform on which threedegrees would sit. The Netgen teammates were known as mavericks who were a bit undisciplined in their process. It was time for more discipline and a culture shift.

The goal of this phase of work was to bring the features of threedegrees into the next version of Messenger. Now the Netgen team members had to pay a lot of attention when they went to a Messenger meeting about platform changes because this information would impact their designs. But the Netgen teammates were also changing Messenger with their new ideas about how to support a group of friends who want to communicate with each other.

The transition was tough. Some of the Netgen members didn't think that the Messenger folks "got" their idea of people getting together first and then choosing an activity. The Messenger folks questioned whether customers would really want this "fluff" product. Jonathan had to pull these disparate groups together. It so happened that in his spare time Jonathan owned and operated a Seattle bar, so he met there with a lot of Messenger people to explain that the Netgen team was sincere about wanting integration. Bonds were built over beer.

Then there were weekly meetings with both Netgen members and Messenger people. Rotating between Seattle and Redmond, the meetings were a chance for everyone to report in on what they were working on. If there was a sticky problem, one person from Netgen and one from Messenger would jointly own the problem and the recommendation. The two groups learned to work together to get the product out the door. Even Bill Gates was a big supporter by this time. He was so enthusiastic about the product that he wanted to move it back to the ISG, where it could be built with a different set of technologies, not peer-to-peer ones. Now Netgen ideology would be integrated into the core ISG, furthering exportation.

As C.J. reflected on the process: "It would have been great if the Netgen team had just grown into some big team and built a great product. The truth is that even though that didn't happen, what did happen was probably more amazing. We really did create an enormous change within the existing organization. We didn't build another organization inside Microsoft; we built a virus, a good virus, and then we infused it into the broader organization"[7] Thus, exportation from the team to the rest of the organization was quite successful. The features of threedegrees, such as circles, became something that key development teams in the ISG incorporated. It is expected to be a foundational element of a new Microsoft release in 2008. Many of those leading this charge are not even aware that this element originated as Netgen technology, but it is on track to ship to over 200 million people. One team member also noted that, "I look at some of the features of Xbox Live and I see a lot of Netgen thinking filtered through a gamer-centric perspective." Here again the Netgen ideas have had an impact on another part of Microsoft.

### *The X-Factors and Exportation*

Extensive ties, expandable tiers, and exchangeable membership all contributed to a successful transition from exploitation to exportation. In fact, the incredible adaptive ability of this X-team is shown in this point: the founder and core leader left the team, but the core work of the team continued. Indeed, the culture of intense ties to outsiders, the shifting of the team's structure and roles, and pulling in new people as needed remained.

Jonathan continued the culture of reaching out to others. With his contact list in hand, he used his connections to coordinate with other groups whose technology and expertise were needed. Jonathan's ties also helped with the integration into Messenger, both with the people who worked on the integration efforts and the top managers who supplied the resources. Jonathan and his teammates also reached out to the Messenger organization to create new ties, whether at the bar or at work, to break down barriers and merge the two groups.

In fact, Jonathan took over control of the core to fill the vacuum formed when Tammy and Melora left. However, other members of the core remained, to continue the development of the product's features, and this helped the team continue along smoothly, despite the turmoil of shifting tasks and membership. This combination of change and stability is also present with the operational tier. Some team members left with Tammy and Melora, while others stayed on to bring the product into

Messenger and, later, back into the ISG. Some folks from Messenger joined the remaining Netgen team members to help with integrating threedegrees onto Messenger's platform and then joined with people from the ISG to move the product to another technology. There have been changes in the outer-net tier as well. Many members of Messenger and the ISG also became outer-net members and then operational members. It's important to note that Netgen team members also dispersed into other groups at Microsoft so that they became core, operational, and outer-net members elsewhere, integrating Netgen ideas into visions.

Exchangeable membership is clearly apparent: as a new set of external contacts and skills are needed within the team, membership shifts. Jonathan Sposata stepped up to head the core, and people from Messenger moved from outer-net into operational positions. One even entered the core. This same shift happened again as the team moved into the ISG.

Was Netgen a success? Most of the members we interviewed gave it an eight or nine out of ten. Why not a ten? First, it took much longer than anyone expected to get a product out the door. Second, the move to Messenger meant that some of the Netgen ideas and features were abandoned. Third, team members excelled at incubation and innovation, but because they were separated from the rest of the organization, it took longer to integrate and ship. In fact, some of the Netgen ideas and features are only now finding a way into the market. Team member ideas were also perhaps a bit ahead of the technology. But another way to think about these elements is that creating a revolution within an organization takes time and perhaps the vehicle of change has to shift over time to make this happen.

On the positive side, however, Netgen succeeded in pioneering a new model for customer inspired software design at Microsoft. It also gave Microsoft a jump start on this idea of online socializing. Most Netgen members further report having had a great experience; it was intense and insane, but they created something new and learned something in the process. They got the ear of top management, and they changed the company's perception of who were leading technology users. They brought their learning back into the company and integrated their ideas into existing products. Furthermore they trained a new set of innovative managers for Microsoft.

X-factors are the enablers of this kind of success, forming a self-reinforcing system. To engage in high levels of external activity, team members must bring to the table outside ties forged in past professional experience. To be responsive to new information and new coordination needs, X-teams have exchangeable membership and a structure featuring multiple tiers and roles. To handle the high coordination demands required for extreme execution, the X-team has a core to structure the team and exchangeable membership that enables a meshing of talent to task. The X-factors cannot work in isolation. They complement one another. Extensive ties enable the team to identify people needed for core, operational, and outer-net positions. Exchangeable membership enables the team to shift its access to particular networks, thus providing the types of ties the team needs at any given point. Although small or new teams may not have all the X-factors, fully developed X-teams usually do. An X-team, therefore, becomes a tiny engine of innovation and execution, moving and shifting as the need arises. In this way, an X-team exhibits distributed leadership by bringing together the talent and resources that the team needs to adapt over time and carrying out, or even shaping, the organization's core goals.

If this sounds difficult, it is. But teams like Netgen show that while the road may be hard and long, the benefits to individuals, teams, and organizations are profound. The good news is that the recipe for translating the theory of X-teams to effective action, as the next chapter shows, can be specified in a series of concrete steps, making the task easier.

# PART III

# How to Build
# Effective X-Teams

# SEVEN

# Tools for X-Teams

## *From Theory to Action*

S UPPOSE THAT YOU ARE A MANAGER charged with creating a team. It might be a product development team, a research team, a sales team, a manufacturing team, a problem-solving team, a committee or task force, or even a top management team. What, exactly, are the tools you would need to craft a high-performing X-team? What would you need to do to jump-start the team's work and enable it to engage in the external activity and extreme execution needed to succeed? What would best help a team move through the phases of exploration, exploitation, and exportation? In short, how can you facilitate a team's ability to engage in distributed leadership in action, pulling together the various resources inside and outside the organization, and up and down the organizational hierarchy, to bring the core mission and strategy of the company to life?

You structure the team to engage in four core steps:

1. Select members and set the stage.

2. Begin exploration.

3. Engage in exploitation.

4. Follow through with exportation.

Each step requires some core tasks, and this chapter will outline concrete checklists that summarize what needs to be done for successfully completing each step. Of course, teams often will not have the time for or require each item on each checklist, so prioritization is key. Also, as we learned in chapter 1 in the case of the two consulting teams, Northwest and Southeast, setting a direction in a team's activity early on can mean the difference between moving toward failure and innovating and adapting to changing environments and the competitive challenges that lie in wait along the road ahead. After setting the stage, team members need to organize themselves for exploration, exploitation, and exportation. Each phase requires scouting, ambassadorship, task coordination, and extreme execution aimed at the core tasks needed at that time. Checklists help teams transition across these phases once the stage has been set.

## Step 1: Select Members and Set the Stage

Think back to our example of Team Fox at Pharmaco. The specific members selected for the team ensured a successful outcome not only because of what they knew when joining the team but because of whom they knew. This enabled the team to wrestle intelligently with emerging challenges and to get the help of others outside the team when those challenges seemed overwhelming.

The ultimate success of an X-team, then, may be determined before the members even meet. The team's composition can make an enormous difference in its ability to carry out ambassadorship, scouting, task coordination, and extreme execution. Most traditional advice in this arena stresses staffing a team with the necessary skills and talents to carry out the core task, complementary personalities and skills, and a motivated set of individuals.[1] And all of this will indeed help the team. But X-teams require an additional ingredient: looking at the social networks or ties of potential team members.

So to the extent that team leaders have some choice in selecting members, they should think about what connections the team is going to need to get started and who might bring access to those connections. In this case, team members are chosen for whom they know—whether it's someone with a PDA full of connections to people within the organization who might offer key expertise, links to top management, access to university researchers doing work that could be useful to the team, or former experience with contractors. Having members with existing ties to the people whom the team needs to partner with can save lots of time and energy in moving the team's work along instead of figuring out how to approach a stranger.

Once team members have been chosen, it is time to get the team started. The beginning of any team is pivotal because it is a time when tensions are high and norms are set that often last throughout the team's life.[2] This is a time of high stress for many team members as they struggle with understanding what role they will play in the team and with fear over whether the team will succeed. This stress, in turn, often results in team members' rushing to get answers and solving problems without adequate thought. This stress also often focuses the team inward, rather than outward, as the X-team view suggests. Finally, this is a time when team members set the stage for how the team will function, so decisions made at this moment will have lasting consequences.

Given these conditions, team members need to use this initial period to get to know one another, create a culture of psychological safety and team reflection, and find out what others know. This is the time to introduce the idea of distributed leadership—the idea that everyone in the team may have to lead at some point and that leadership will be shared with others outside the team. This is the time to set the team's focus outward and to create activities that will help alleviate the stress that members may exhibit in unproductive ways.

---

## KEY TASKS FOR SELECTING MEMBERS AND SETTING THE STAGE

1. Select the right team members by . . .
   - Generating a list of the people who are candidates for team membership because they bring the necessary content and process skills, personality, and motivation to help the team succeed
   - Generating a list of the most important people the team will need to interact with over the course of its life
   - Finding out which of these candidates has strong or weak ties to key individuals
   - Choosing the candidates with the best mix of content and process skills as well as external ties

2. Create a culture of team success by . . .
   - Getting to know team members
   - Meeting in a setting in which the team will not be disturbed
   - Having members introduce themselves and talk about backgrounds
   - Having members talk about their strengths and weaknesses and what they bring to the team, including both task expertise and personality traits (e.g., "I hate working on computers" or "I like everything to be very clear and organized")

- Discussing members' best and worst team experiences—that is, what people want to create in this team and what they definitely want to avoid

- Generating a list of people team members know who may be of some help to the team now or in the future

- Finding out about people's schedules and work habits and determining the best ways and times to meet and stay in touch

3. Build psychological safety and team reflection by . . .

- Setting explicit norms that encourage candidness in the team

- Encouraging all members to ask for help and to help others

- Knowing when to let others in the team take the lead

- Reacting nondefensively when disagreement occurs and seeking a solution

- Modeling risk taking by discussing fears and new ideas

- Building in time during every meeting for members to reflect on what is going on in the team and how they feel about it

4. Find out what other team members know by . . .

- "Mapping" the expertise in the team, including members' knowledge areas and networks, activities they like to perform (e.g., making PowerPoint presentations), and key parts of the task that they have done before

- Finding out what other tasks members might enjoy and encouraging their exploration

- Encouraging knowledge sharing in the team by asking questions and getting reports, and establishing this as a continuous process

Not every team member will be as comfortable as others in opening up and talking about their experiences, feelings, and desires for the future. Cultural differences often play a role in people's comfort level as well, and teams should work to understand those differences while simultaneously making it easier for people to participate. Note the difficulties that Gerhard Koepke—the project manager whose predicament introduced chapter 4—had in ensuring that team members shared information that was critical to making his plant a profitable venture. Meeting over a meal, finding some relaxing activity, or introducing humor when possible will all help alleviate stress and anxiety. Then it is time to organize exploration work so that team members can feel as if they are making progress.

## Step 2: Begin Exploration

The first phase of an X-team's work is exploration. This is a time for team members to explore their task, their environment, the customer, the technology, and the competition. Members need to suspend their prior views of the situation and look at the world with new eyes—to explore their new terrain so that they're able to describe it, to find hidden opportunities as well as dangerous traps. Members of Team Fox did just that when they found their hidden gem, a molecule that eventually became a blockbuster drug, through a subsidiary in another country. Team members also need to pull on the expertise around them and open up a dialogue with top management so that vision and implementation can be aligned. The Razr team built some of its new technology on ideas that others had discarded and found a match between the team's product and senior management's desire to change Motorola's image. Exploration leads to discovery, to new understandings of what the team faces, and thus facilitates later action.

In the language of leadership, this is the time for intense sensemaking and relating. In the language of X-teams, those activities correspond to high levels of scouting, ambassadorship, and extreme execution, and the beginning of task coordination. As the Big Bank group at BellCo discovered, exploration is an opportunity to learn about the problem that the team has to solve and the context in which it has to operate. This is the time to realize that there will be no magic corporate guidelines to provide the answers (you may have to find them yourself) or that you need to develop new working relationships with groups you've never interacted with before. This is the time to really understand what customers want—for example, systems solutions rather than stand-alone products—and to determine where the competition is.

For a team to be effective during this phase of activity, members need to draw on many different kinds of data and points of view. They need to learn from hard data and observation and take into account their own gut feelings and the ideas of people who hold opposing perspectives. The goal is to describe the task so that members understand it fully and deeply and can communicate it to others.

Sensemaking and relating, scouting, ambassadorship, and task coordination require that the team identifies all the different people who will have an impact on, or be influenced by, the team task. Seeking far and wide for those with expertise, power, advice, and support—and even those who may want to sabotage the team's work—is important. Figuring out what these people want, how they feel, what they need, what they expect, and what they may be willing to settle for is as important as simultaneously figuring out what the team members want to accomplish and how those goals will fit into the identified opportunities and constraints. The exploration phase, with its emphasis on sensemaking and relating, can be broken down into key scouting, ambassadorial, and task coordination tasks, as well as extreme execution.

The key for a team at the start of its work is to create a plan that will allocate responsibility for these pivotal tasks (see figure 7-1). It should focus on what has to be done, who has to do it, and when it must be finished. The work plan should also account for who has major responsibility and who will assist. The plan also needs to include key meeting dates and milestones for the team.

**FIGURE 7-1**

## X-team work plan

| What? Key tasks | When? Due date | Who? Key person/assisting person |
|---|---|---|
| 1. | | |
| 2. | | |
| 3. | | |
| 4. | | |
| Next meeting dates: | | |

## KEY TASKS FOR EXPLORATION

### SCOUTING

1. Investigate the organizational terrain

   - Investigate the problem, issue, or opportunity. Find out how others in the firm view the team's task, and probe to learn what they are expecting, thinking, and feeling about the task. View the task and the organization through different lenses (e.g., strategic, political, and cultural) to get a nuanced and complete picture.

   - Search for other teams within your organization that have engaged in similar tasks and learn from them.

2. Investigate customers, competitors, and current trends

- Try to discover customer needs and trends. Work with current customers as well as those who have opted for the competition, those who are cutting-edge innovators, and those who are more traditional.[a] Examine current needs and those that might be expected in the future.

- Scan the environment inside and out for new ideas, practices, or technologies that may be adapted to the team's needs.

- Find out what competing firms or groups are doing on similar projects.

3. Investigate yourselves

- Discuss how each member views the team and the task. Figure out what points of view are missing and what biases exist within the team that may limit its ability to see all perspectives.

- Discuss what each member wants to get out of this phase of the project and whether the team can meet these needs.

During this phase of scouting activity, it might be helpful to create and update a map of who might have information, expertise, and resources that the team may need. Also, create a summary of what the team learns during this phase so that everyone has access to what has happened and members are all on the same page.

## AMBASSADORSHIP

1. Link to strategic initiatives and get buy-in

- Communicate with top managers in the organization to determine key strategic initiatives. Then link the team goals to these initiatives, either by aligning them to these initiatives or by working to shift the initiatives.

- Get buy-in from senior-level managers for the team's direction and plans. Talk to these managers to solicit suggestions on how the team's ideas can be improved and what would be most helpful to the managers. Ask for support for the team's work and what the team would have to do to obtain and maintain that support.

2. Lobby for the team's interests

- Persuade others that the team's ideas are important and need to be supported. Try to create a network of support throughout the top layers of management.

- Crusade for those things that the team members feel most strongly about. Even if there is some resistance, work for those things that team members feel most passionate about doing.

3. Cultivate allies and protect against adversaries

- Find out who supports the team's activities, and work to shore up and foster this support. Ask supporters for help in gaining access to resources, identifying important sources of information and new contacts, and shaping the project.

- Work to protect the team from political adversaries by identifying who they are, trying to find ways to win them over, or if that is not possible, attempting to contain the damage that they can do. Solicit the support of allies in this process.

At the end of the exploration phase, teams should have a good idea of who their top management supporters and sponsors are and a plan to follow up with them. At those follow-up sessions, team members should be prepared to provide progress reports, get feedback, and continue to solicit support. These sessions should include not only discussions of what the team is trying to do but also how the team should meet the political challenges that are coming its way.

**TASK COORDINATION**

1. Identify dependencies

   • Identify those individuals and groups, inside and outside
     the company, who have something that the team might
     need to do its task (e.g., know-how, expertise, services),
     and start discussions about how the team might work with
     these other groups.

   • Identify those individuals and groups that might take over
     the team's work when it is finished. Get input from these
     people about what they might need from the team to make
     the transition easier and to avoid surprises (e.g., the compo-
     nent that the team wants to use in design will make manu-
     facturing much more difficult).

   • Identify people from outside the team who might be called on
     to join the team to facilitate interdependent work. For exam-
     ple, an engineering team might want someone from finance
     or manufacturing to join the group for some period to help
     prepare contracts or design components that will ease coordi-
     nation with these other functions later in the process.

   • Put together a plan and schedule for how the team will work
     with other groups.

2. Get feedback from other groups

   • Ask other groups that will work with the team for their reac-
     tions and suggestions about what the team is planning.

   • Brainstorm with these other groups about how the collabora-
     tion might best work. Establish a culture of innovation in
     which each partner suggests new solutions to the problems
     of interdependence.

3. Convince, negotiate, and cajole

- Work to convince, cajole, and negotiate with other interdependent groups to get support for commitments now and in
  the future. These other groups may have different incentive
  plans or may not be motivated to shift what they are doing
  now to work with the team. Think about how to change
  their minds.

- Reward other groups when they do help the team meet its
  goals. If another group offers to design a piece of software or
  suggests a new design for the team, send its members a pizza
  or offer to do something for them in return.

At the end of the exploration phase, an effective X-team will have
identified its task as well as the people outside the team who will be
needed to help the team meet its goals. The team will have received
feedback, worked to gain cooperation and collaboration from other
groups, and found ways to motivate and reward the work of external
contributors.


## EXTREME EXECUTION

While team members are gearing up for extreme execution during the
exploration phase, they should not forget that they are always following the guidelines set up at the start for creating a culture of psychological safety and team reflection, as stated at the beginning of this
chapter. They are also continuously updating their information on who
knows what and what each team member brings to the table. Without
this underlying culture of support, learning, and knowledge about the
other members, extreme execution is difficult to create. These are the
fundamentals that create trust, without which a team struggles. Once
such fundamentals are established and maintained, the team can move
on to the core tasks of extreme execution.

1. Set norms

Norms refer to expectations about acceptable behavior. These are the written or unwritten rules that guide team members' behavior. All norms that are set during exploration are initial guesses about the best way for the team to operate and may only apply for this first phase of work. As such, team members must realize that these norms and roles may need to be renegotiated as time goes by. But the team has to start somewhere.

- Start by setting some basic norms about how the team will operate, including how much time to put into team activity, what level of quality is acceptable, how often to meet, how to distribute work, and how to make decisions. Norms must also be set to maintain psychological safety and reflection by reiterating rules established during the set-up of the team.

- Create a norm of periodic integrative meetings to pull together all the information and work that has been done by members. Such meetings help members decide how to integrate and interpret information and plan the next stage of action. The need for integration is particularly heightened when team members have been out meeting with different organizational members, customers, and suppliers, and coming up with new views of the task.

- Set a norm of participatory decision making, such that different member viewpoints are aired and considered. Not everyone's ideas can make it into the final decision, however, so a norm of transparency in letting everyone know how and why a decision is made helps keep members committed to the decisions that are made.

- Create heuristics, which are norms around the team's key operating rules. Whether the heuristic is "Customers always

come first, even if we might lose some money" or "Make decisions as quickly as possible without compromising safety,"
these rules help members make choices between options that
might all seem attractive.

3. Use tools for extreme execution

- Create shared timelines. These shared timelines document
  key deadlines and milestones, as well as time for reflection
  and critical decisions. Shared timelines enable each team
  member to work on his or her own schedule while ensuring
  that individual work comes together at key moments to produce team output and progress.

- Set up information management systems that enable the team
  to track the information that is coming in, decisions that are
  made, and progress on the task at hand. These systems might
  be quite sophisticated or merely blogs. Whatever the technology, ease of use is key, or else busy team members are unlikely
  to use it.

4. Allocate roles

Roles are specific activities taken on by particular members.
Here again roles that are set up at the start of a team might not
work as the task changes or as people's talents, interests, and
motivations no longer mesh with the work at hand.

- Allocate roles that facilitate ongoing teamwork. This might include someone to chair and organize meetings (this may be a
  rotating role), a facilitator to make sure that people are participating and that the team stays on course, and a project manager who makes sure that people are sticking to the work plan.
  Boundary spanners who work with particular outside groups
  (e.g., contractors, top management, or key customers) help
  keep confusion down.

- Allocate key X-team roles. Decide who will be the core members that will carry the team's history and identity, manage across the different tiers, and keep the entire team focused on core tasks. Decide who will be operational members—that is, the people who will carry out the work of selling the product, designing the software, exploring an oil field, or testing a new drug. Finally, figure out who will be the outer-net members who join the team for a limited time to do a specific piece of work. Remember that people can play more than one role at a given moment and that these roles can rotate.

a. E. von Hippel, *The Sources of Innovation* (Oxford: Oxford University Press, 1988).

---

By the end of exploration, the team should be set up for extreme execution. Members come to trust each other and work together easily, engaging in genuine dialogue and managing conflicts. They will have set themselves up for deep exploration of the situation at hand as well as learning how to work together to open up a world of new possibilities.

## Step 3: Engage in Exploitation

When team members move from opening up possibilities and looking at their task from multiple vantage points to selecting one direction and making it happen—they have entered exploitation, the second phase of an X-team's work. Now members must shift from the realm of possibilities to creating one reality, from brainstorming about what can be done to actually doing it. As such, the team has to refocus its activity and move into a phase of implementation and execution. For instance, this was the stage at which Netgen decided to narrow the scope of the team's project and get a software product out the door for beta testing with real customers. This was the time to move from dreaming about what was possible to building a concrete prototype for the marketplace.

In the language of leadership, this is a time for intense visioning and inventing. First, team members need to commit to a vision of what it is that they want to create. It is a time for them to review all the ideas, data, and perspectives that have come from the exploration phase and decide how they can make the most impact on the organization. They have to decide what they most care about and want to achieve. Then they need to invent the processes and structures necessary to make the vision a reality. They need to learn from others and create their own innovative ways to make their product or market their wares. They need to do some rapid prototyping and test what works so that they can quickly iterate and improve during this phase of activity.

From an X-team perspective, scouting, ambassadorship, task coordination, and extreme execution continue, but their direction and levels change. Scouting shifts from looking at the task from multiple perspectives to looking for who has done this task before, what those other people or groups learned, and how the team can build on what those others know. Ambassadorship becomes a less dominant task because, instead of finding and building buy-in and support, the team simply has to maintain the support it has. Task coordination, however, will gain in prominence as members work with other groups throughout the organization to move their product along. These other groups need to be motivated and monitored. And extreme execution becomes ever-more complex as the team grows in size and members work with people inside and outside the team. As Netgen's experience illustrated, this might mean having to add new members and to change the roles that existing members play.

As in the exploration phase, an effective X-team continues to work on a team plan, outlining key tasks and determining who will take them on and when they must be completed. Key milestones and meeting dates are agreed on, and the plan is updated as the team completes these milestones.

## KEY TASKS FOR EXPLOITATION

Since some of the steps in exploitation are a continuation of steps from exploration, we have focused here on changes and new elements of scouting, ambassadorship, task coordination, and extreme execution.

### SCOUTING

1. Investigate the organizational terrain

   - With a specific output in mind, it is important to get input and reactions from the key stakeholders within the firm and suggestions about what might be done to improve on the idea and its implementation.

   - Search out other teams within the organization that have engaged in similar tasks and learn from them. What solutions did they try? What were the results? Who worked with the team? Were these satisfying partnerships? Why or why not? How can the team build on this knowledge?

2. Investigate customers, competitors, and current trends

   - As solutions and products are created, test the customer reactions. What do customers like? What don't they like? What changes would they make? Interviews, focus groups, and beta testing with customers can help refine the product and assure success in the marketplace.

   - Scan the environment for ways to structure the team and engage in innovative practices that will help the team operate more effectively and efficiently in getting the task done. Adapt these to the needs of the team.

   - Look not only at competitors in the same industry but also at those outside. Perhaps people in the auto industry know more about standardization and platforms than do people in your industry, while product design firms know more about innovation. If you are trying to improve these aspects of your organization, you might get more sophisticated ideas by looking further afield.

- Search for market and technological advances in academia and the consulting world to come up with new ideas for your product and how to make it a reality.

3. Investigate yourselves

- Discuss whether each member is committed to the new direction that the team has taken. If members are not committed to the new vision and mode of inventing, discuss what can be done to bring the work of the team in line with member needs and goals.

- Discuss whether team members believe that this solution is the best way to tackle the task at hand. If not, continue to work to create a motivated team.

## AMBASSADORSHIP

Ambassadorship continues during exploitation, albeit at a lower level.

1. Link to strategic initiatives and get buy-in

- Team members continue to align with top management, represent the team's interests, and cultivate allies and protect against adversaries. The key difference here is that the team is typically not seeking new support but rather reinforcing and maintaining the support it already has. The only exception is if changes in the task or sponsor relationship warrant seeking out new sponsorship opportunities.

- The team will have to continue to report in on progress that it is making and check to make sure that the product it is designing is still aligned with strategic directions.

- Team members might also want to show how they have taken into account prior suggestions from top management about what the team should do.

2. Lobby for the team's interests

- Team members will have to continue to ensure that the team's interests are in the minds of top management. Periodic meetings expressing what the team needs and what role management can play in helping the team get resources and sponsorship continue throughout the team's life.

3. Cultivate allies and protect against adversaries

- As the team progresses, adversaries may get more aggressive and try to stop its work. Team members may have to seek help from allies and top management supporters in countering this opposition.

- Allies must continuously be cultivated, or the team risks losing the fruits of its labor.

## TASK COORDINATION

During exploitation, task coordination often increases. While creating a new product or service, the team often has to work with other groups inside and outside the organization. For example, the Big Bank team had to coordinate its sales activities with the technical people who actually designed the product as well as the people in installation who had to make sure that the product worked at the customer site. The Netgen team's members had to work with people throughout Microsoft who would help them develop parts of their software, like the music and video components. They also needed to integrate their features with those created by other groups and to align schedules with several groups. Add to this the need to integrate with groups outside the organization, like the customers who were testing the beta models, and task coordination can take on a large portion of people's time and energy.

During this phase the key components of task coordination shift a bit.

1. Identify and create plans for managing dependencies

- The major shift during exploitation is that the set of dependencies differs from those of earlier phases. Now the team needs to work with those groups that can help it actually implement its ideas. This means figuring out how the team can work with these groups—shared timelines, integrative meetings, assigning liaison people, and creating shared work plans are all possibilities.

- Other groups might be added that are needed to provide new expertise or information or to take on some aspect of the task that is outside the boundaries of what the team can do.

- As the team begins to work closely with these other groups, its members need to figure out common schedules, agree on mutual commitments, and check to see that those commitments are maintained.

- The team needs to continue to build a culture of innovation and cooperation with these other groups so that new modes of working together can be invented and conflict minimized.

2. Get feedback

- Once the team has active working relationships with other groups, there should be periodic check-ins to see how well the relationships are working and what can be done to improve them.

3.  Convince, negotiate, and cajole

    • Motivating these other groups in creative ways continues to be a part of the team's major activities.

    • Often greater commitment from these other groups is needed during this phase of activity, so team members may need to spend more time on working with others and to get help from senior management to ensure cooperation. Relying on strong ties with other groups also helps ensure commitment.

The goal of exploitation is to make the team's dreams a reality, and this reality may be improved even more by the work of others in the organization who help make it happen. (If technical design and installation can be convinced to deliver to the customer on time, not only the team but also the organization wins by pulling ahead in the competitive marketplace.) Task coordination helps involve those other groups.

**EXTREME EXECUTION**

Extreme execution during exploitation will require reinforcing the guidelines set up at the start of the team for creating psychological safety and team reflection. This is a good time to check that such a culture has truly been created and to determine whether any changes are necessary to bolster these core values and activities. In fact, as the team changes gears from an emphasis on sensemaking and relating to visioning and inventing, members need to rethink their norms, tools, and roles. The team has to be set up to engage in a different set of tasks, and its old way of operating might not fit this new way of working. Also, a new set of people may come into the team who are more concerned with execution than brainstorming—more focused on milestones, budgets, and schedules than on dreaming about what is possible. This signals a change in how the team must operate within its borders.[a]

1. Set norms

- The team will still have to set norms about how it will operate. However, prior decisions about how often to meet, how work will be distributed, and how decisions get made may need to change. With a clear product or process defined as the final product, and some idea about whether rapid prototyping and feedback cycles are needed, the team now moves its operations around how to actually make the product a reality. Each person's job in making this happen has to be defined, and meetings are set to match key milestones in the process.

- Integrative meetings are still needed, but these might have to change to include those outside groups that are also contributing to the product design and may need to alternate between progress reports, problems that need to be solved, and new ways of advancing the work. These meetings need to focus not only on what subgroups are doing but also on how they are coordinating. Meetings may need to be set up for different combinations of core, operational, and outer-net members. Participatory decision making will need to continue as the team works to make key milestones and deadlines.

- Team members may also need to create new heuristics to deal with their new work. Heuristics around how to balance speed and quality, how to determine the mix of things that the team will do itself and things that others will do, and how to balance meeting the demands of key stakeholders—such as customers, marketers, top management, and contractors—will need to be determined.

2. Use tools for extreme execution

- The tools for extreme execution, like shared timelines and in-formation management systems, will need to be reconfigured for implementation. Chances are that these tools will get more complex and that more people will use them. When many people and groups are involved, such as in the building of a new car or the development of a new technique for extracting oil from under the sea, these tools may even form a core com-petitive advantage.

- For other types of teams, these tools may actually get simpler. For example, a team writing code might have had to meet often and use tools to pull its many ideas together during ex-ploration. Once a design is chosen, however, the code may be divided up into sections that are easily put together. Under these conditions the need for coordination tools decreases.

3. Allocate roles

- Role allocation will also need to change. In many instances the people who are best at creation and exploration are not the same people who are best at implementation and execu-tion. Thus, the people who are facilitating team meetings and serving as project manager may have to change. Also, different people might have to move into the core and play different roles than they did before. With the addition of new outer-net members, the core might also need to play a greater role in managing and coordinating the team's work.

a. See C. J. G. Gersick, "Time and Transition in Work Teams," *Academy of Management Journal* 31 (1988): 9–41; J. R. Hackman and R. Wageman, "A Theory of Team Coaching," *Academy of Management Review* 30 (2005): 269–287.

In short, many of the same tasks hold for exploitation as for exploration; but their nature, scope, and direction change, and the team moves from deciding what to do to trying to become better at figuring out how to do it. But by the end of exploitation, the team should have some product—whether it's an actual product or a process or an idea—and the next challenge is getting that product integrated into the rest of the organization or out to the market.

## Step 4: Follow Through with Exportation

Moving from exploitation to exportation means turning outward again, to export the project to the rest of the organization. For Netgen, for example, this meant changing the geographic focus from Seattle to Redmond and integrating its product into Microsoft Messenger. For the Merrill team this meant focusing on how to convince top management—and, in particular, Dow Kim—to make its idea a corporate reality and then helping the new managers of the distressed equity desk move quickly up the learning curve. The goal of exportation is to transfer the excitement, motivation, and tacit knowledge of the team to those people who will take on the next phase of the team's work or who will bring the team's work to other parts of the organization. Exportation is also a time for the team to reflect on what it has done and what it has learned so that it can pass on this information to others. Here again the team will have to put together a work plan, including key tasks, task assignments, and deadlines. But now the focus is primarily external: how can we make this an organizational product, not just something that the team is excited about?

## KEY TASKS FOR EXPORTATION

### SCOUTING

1. Investigate the organizational terrain

   - Find the key people who must be convinced to continue the team's work. Try to discover what arguments, types of presentations, data, and style most appeal to these people.

   - Find out how others in the organization doing similar work have succeeded in handing off their work to others. What have they done, and how can the team build on that knowledge?

2. Investigate customers, competitors, and current trends

   - Find out how customers, competitors, and other relevant outside groups respond to the team's product. Make changes based on this information.

3. Investigate yourselves

   - Discuss which team members might want to continue the team's work after the project is over. Think about how this might be accomplished.

   - Discuss any inhibitions that team members might have about letting go of "their" product and giving it to others. Figure out a way to get closure for the team and help people move on.

Key to scouting in this phase is determining who the key players are who will make the decision about the transfer and how the team can best influence those people. Another core task is looking at how other teams have handled the handoff to others and what has been most successful.

## AMBASSADORSHIP

If the team has been active in its ambassadorship all along, then the final presentation or transfer should go quite easily. If communication and buy-in has been maintained, then upper management should already have signed off on the idea, and this final transition is more of a public display of an agreed-on outcome. Then the team needs to garner top management support in making sure that the group taking over realizes that this work is a corporate priority. If the transition involves a very different part of the organization, then it may be necessary to garner new sponsorship.

1. Link to strategic initiatives and get buy-in

   - In preparing for the final presentation or report, or getting ready to shift ownership of the product to another group, it helps to have upper-level support. It is useful to have allies and sponsors present at such events to show their support, but if this is not possible then other kinds of endorsements (e.g., quotations, video clips, or actual physical examples of products that executives liked) also come in handy.

   - Consider what the top managers think is most important, the way they like data presented, and the best way to make the case so that it wins the hearts and minds of those with the resources and power to make such a transfer possible.

2. Lobby for the team's interests

   - Team members should be out presenting the team's point of view and convincing top management of the importance of bringing the team's work into the organization.

3. Cultivate allies and protect against adversaries

   - A whole new set of allies and adversaries may arise when the team's product moves into the rest of the organization. Try to figure out who these people are in advance, and work with others to bring adversaries on board and to cultivate new allies. Netgen faced this dilemma as it shifted its work to be part of Microsoft Messenger.

## TASK COORDINATION

1. Identify dependencies and convince, negotiate, and cajole

- Task coordination during exportation is most important with those groups that will take on the next phase of the work. No group's members like to have something imposed on them, and so the main task of the team is to help other groups understand why the team has passion for its product, why it did what it did, and why it wants this other group to continue the work.

- Team members can offer their support in helping with the transfer—whether it's passing along files, information, know-how, or simply background information.

- Expressing excitement about what the product can do and why it has been so important can be the most effective tool in spreading excitement to this other group. Without this excitement sometimes transfer does not occur.

## EXTREME EXECUTION

Extreme execution during exportation is about coordinating a shift to sales mode.

1. Set norms

- The team will still have to set norms about how the team will operate. But as in the shift from exploration to exploitation, the shift to exportation means that prior decisions about how often the team will meet, how work will be distributed, and how decisions get made may need to change to fit the task at hand.

- Integrative meetings are still needed, but the objective shifts. It is now about organizing to give the product the best marketing and send-off possible. This might involve organizing a display of the product or some demonstration of what the product can do.

2. Use tools for extreme execution

- The tools for extreme execution, like shared timelines and information management systems, will need to be reconfigured for getting others excited about the team's product.

- Other tools might have to be added. This may involve fancy PowerPoint presentations or the creation of an easy-to-read report. Pictures, stories, data, quotations, and video clips can all help make the case for the team's product.

3. Allocate roles

- New skills may be needed and new roles allocated to find the people who excel at exportation activities. The team, for example, might need to add some new members who excel at marketing or who have contacts in the groups that will ultimately be taking over the management of the project. Whatever it takes, it is worth it to move the product along and have the team end with a sense of accomplishment.

4. Reflect on lessons learned

- A key thing that team members need to do is to record what they have learned. This might involve an off-site to reflect on what has been learned or simply creating a list of team reflections.

- The team might want to figure out a way to pass its learning on to others, whether by publishing its ideas or making them available to the next set of teams to embark on a similar task.

- Following the common military practice of an after-action review, or debriefing, this is the time to focus on what worked, what did not work, and what might be done differently the next time.

---

Once exportation is finished, the team is done. Yet it is important to recognize the work of all the people involved and to give people a chance to frame their experience, celebrate, and mark the end of this job and the move to another. Parties, mock graduations, dinners, roasts, and other occasions are all good venues.[3]

This chapter offers guidelines for individual X-teams and shows precisely how teams can get through exploration, exploitation, and exportation. But what if a manager wants to create a set of X-teams? What if he or she wants an X-team program to make X-teams an ongoing part of organizational operations? The next chapter investigates how this structure of distributed leadership and innovation can be created and maintained.

# EIGHT

# Crafting an Infrastructure for Innovation

## *The X-Team Program*

W E'VE SHOWN HOW to create an X-team and provided checklists to help in its development. But suppose you are a CEO, or the director of a large division, or the head of human resources, or a manager in R&D, and you don't want to create just one X-team. What if you want to create a set of X-teams that provides an infrastructure of innovation, multiple X-teams that create innovative products and ideas year after year and eventually reshape the way your organization functions? This calls for an X-team program—such as those developed at both Merrill Lynch and BP.

### BP's X-Team Program

In September 2004, the members of seven X-teams from BP (known as Interterm teams inside the company) spent half a day presenting the work that they had done over the previous year to a group of BP management and staff and MIT faculty. As presentation followed presentation, the excitement grew. What these teams had done in one year was truly extraordinary. They had invented new processes and architectures to improve project management at BP. These seven teams were the second group (or "cadre") of thirty major project leaders to go through the BP/MIT Projects Academy, whose primary sponsors were BP's Ellis Armstrong, group vice president for exploration and production, and Tony Meggs, group vice president in technology. The Projects Academy is a yearlong program in which senior project managers spend six weeks at MIT and work on Interterm-team projects between academic sessions to develop their leadership capability, technical excellence, and business acumen.

The members of these X-teams were senior project leaders who manage multi-million-dollar oil and gas projects for BP around the world. Converging on Cambridge, Massachusetts, they came from Azerbaijan, Abu Dhabi, Algeria, Holland, Indonesia, Russia, Trinidad, the United States, the United Kingdom, and Vietnam. When they arrived in Cambridge for their first sessions a year earlier, many of them did not know each other. But after a couple of weeks together, they had formed a close-knit group. Their task: to first investigate and then suggest ways to improve an aspect of how BP runs its major projects. The vehicle to carry out this task: a set of X-teams made up of these project leaders and launched before they returned to their respective countries and jobs.

Now, one year later, these senior project managers were poised and confident as they brought out their PowerPoint presentations and visual displays and demonstrated what they had learned through their study at MIT and through their action learning in X-teams. They had created new ways to manage the huge multi-million-dollar projects that BP runs around the world. Some teams offered innovative new management systems and processes, new ways to contract with suppliers, new ways to choose and evaluate major projects, and suggestions on how to staff them. Other teams suggested new ways to set up joint ventures, to structure projects, to gain value from technology, and to standardize across projects to get time and cost savings. These ideas, teams projected, could save millions. And, in fact, some of them have already been implemented with cost-saving results, and management is moving ahead on many others.

For example, one team's members were interested in how organizational structure could be changed to optimize delivery and improve project performance. Through scouting, team members discovered a specific project that was under way where they could test their ideas. Using a new technique that helps analyze what information needs to flow to which people given the task at hand, the team found that 45 percent of the communications needed to manage the project fell outside the key functional teams that made up the core structure of the project. With this analysis they examined alternative designs and found that by creating a particular kind of multifunctional team, they could funnel through it the key communications and improve efficiency. The analysis also enabled the team to consider alternative project pathways and key decision points. Ambassadorship with project leaders enabled the team to implement some of its ideas, resulting in greater efficiencies and avoiding many weeks of rework time. The team recommended using the analysis on other projects, and these savings have been multiplied many times over.

But BP's gains in setting up this X-team program—consisting of one to two cadres of thirty participants each year—go beyond specific projects. Individuals report feeling more connected to their counterparts in other parts of the world, having a broader sense of the company and how it operates, and having more knowledge and experience about what it takes to make major change happen. These individuals say that they approach their work differently—understanding problems more deeply before attempting to move into focused problem solving. Furthermore, through this cadre system (the BP-MIT alliance is now working with its seventh cadre), the corporation has created an infrastructure of innovation in which new ideas are emerging each year and in which knowledge is building from one year to the next, and new networks of connection are developed.

Graduates of the program also know how to create, and work in, an X-team. Their conclusion? X-teams work. As members of the joint-venture team (Chris Cox [Abu Dhabi], John O'Brien [Russia], Richard Lynch [Angola], Jack Brinley [China], and Paul Bailey [United Kingdown], plus mentors in Houston [Jim Breson] and Boston [Michael Scott-Morton]), wrote, "We gazed into the glistening pool of knowledge and we were shocked to see our team in the reflection—You can teach old dogs new tricks!"[1] That particular team's journey started with some real doubts that were overcome as they worked together during the year. They wrote in their final report, for example: "What do London Heathrow; Abu Dhabi, United Arab Emirates; Luanda, Angola; In Amenas, Algeria; Shanghai, China; Moscow, Russia; Sudbury on Thames and London, England; and Boston, Massachusetts all have in common besides unique cultures and interesting food? The answer: Each location represents the virtual and occasional face-to-face meeting points for our project team. This global expanse and ability to interact seemed like a 'bridge too far' in our kick-off meeting, but through the effective use of communication tools, . . . the development of personal relationships based on trust and respect, team recognition of individual strength and diversity of each team member, seeking and using a broad network of internal and external joint venture experts, we have succeeded as an X-team."

The BP folks had leadership workshops and a lot of other classes, including systems dynamics, value-chain economics, risk analysis, and complex systems management. They spent a total of six weeks at MIT for education in diverse disciplines designed to meet their needs as leaders of major projects all over the world. Do you need all of this to create X-teams? No. One of us created another series of X-teams at Merrill Lynch in the context of a learning engagement that consisted of two classroom days, DVD lectures, and remote office hours.

## Merrill Lynch's X-Team Program

In July 2004, ten Merrill Lynch X-teams—created four months before in a special MIT Sloan School of Management executive education
program taught for Merrill Lynch, called the Merrill Lynch-MIT Academy—congregated in a conference room in a tall office building on Wall
Street. Teams represented different areas of Merrill Lynch—including
debt, equity, research, and investment management—and members came
from Barcelona, Chicago, London, New York, and Tokyo. Their task for
the day was to present their ideas for new products to executive vice
president and president of global markets and investment banking Dow
Kim and a group of his direct reports, many of whom were the teams'
sponsors.

In typical X-team fashion, these teams had carried out scouting with
customers and analysts, they had engaged in ambassadorship by bringing their ideas to top management to get input and reactions, and they
had exhibited task coordination by linking up with teams that had
worked on similar projects and got them to help the team. The Merrill
Lynch team described in chapter 5 is an example of a team that went
through exploration, exploitation, and exportation to come up with the
idea of a distressed equity desk that sold shares in companies coming
out of bankruptcy. This new structure not only made money for the
company, but it also brought together two units that had not worked together before.

The result? At Merrill Lynch, X-teams have been busy creating everything from new interest rate volatility indexes to a foreign-exchange
hedge-fund index. But they have done more than create innovative new
products. X-teams have pushed Merrill Lynch into a whole new business, created synergies across organizational units, and even gained public recognition for the leadership abilities of graduates of the program.
People who have been through the Merrill Lynch-MIT program report a

greater understanding of the business and a much better idea of what it takes to create a new product in the Merrill Lynch culture. And let's not forget the $3 million that one team made before the course was even over.

At Merrill Lynch, the initiation of the X-teams approach in an already established program highlights its impact. For several years Merrill Lynch had been running the Merrill Lynch-MIT investments course with Professor Andrew W. Lo. With Professor Lo's cutting-edge concepts about investment theory and financial risk, his well-thought-out course, and his entertaining lecture style, the course was very popular. A number of great new product ideas had come out of the project teams launched during the course. There was one big problem, however: the great new projects were not being implemented. Enter X-teams. After adding X-teams to the program in 2003, three projects were implemented, and by 2005, the number was up to nine—which included every single project idea. It turns out that new ways of thinking and new ideas for products are good, but put them together with a vehicle for implementation and excellent execution like X-teams, and the combination is unbeatable.

In short, X-team programs resulted in an ongoing stream of innovative products and processes, as well as a forum for leadership development for next-generation leaders at both BP and Merrill Lynch. When pressed for what made a difference to their performance, team members pointed to the very same attributes that we have been talking about: networking and sponsorship, scouting and sensemaking, finding out what other groups in the company were doing, asking questions and getting ideas from inside and outside the company, and using deadlines and milestones to coordinate work. These teams changed membership over time, inviting in experts as necessary. The key was to organize a set of X-teams, give them some clear goals and procedures, provide scheduled deliverables and faculty feedback, prepare executives to be sponsors, and let the teams go.

But what motivates a company to even consider creating multiple X-teams, and what are the key success factors in implementing them?

## Creating an X-Team Program: The Why and How for Top Management

We've found that companies often choose to create an X-team program because they face a common set of dilemmas that they hope X-teams can solve. While we have spoken about these various dilemmas in earlier parts of this book, we've put them together here to highlight what motivates a leader to create an X-team program. Companies see X-teams as a way to improve business as usual, but they are also an instrument of change, a mechanism to institutionalize innovation, and a way to link a firm's top, middle, and lower levels so that they are all moving in the same direction. X-teams are also a structure to engage in distributed leadership.

While these outcomes can come from individual X-teams, an X-team program does more to institutionalize these changes, creating a broader and deeper impact on organizational culture and practices. In short, X-team programs help managers solve four basic dilemmas that plague organizations today.

*Dilemma 1: How can we innovate and gain competitive advantage when our people are already overworked with day-to-day activities?*

More and more companies are finding that the key to competitive advantage is innovation. It is a tough world out there—resources are stretched, margins are down, organizations have already cut out all the fat and some of the muscle. Since most companies have improved the quality of their products and services, quality no longer offers a competitive advantage, and it's become harder to win in the marketplace through efficiency and economies of scale than ever before. Innovation offers the only route to success. Both BP and Merrill Lynch found that business as usual was not offering the opportunities to have even more client impact, more innovative practices, and more integration across different parts of the companies. They needed to mobilize their organizations to act and think in new ways.

But innovation is easier said than done. With flattened organizational hierarchies many employees are working harder than ever just to get their regular jobs done. There is no slack to think about new products and processes or to reflect on what is working and what needs to be changed. What managers need is a mechanism that provides the time and structure for new ideas and change—a new infrastructure that will move them ahead in an ever-more competitive environment. Enter X-teams.

Organizations can set up X-team programs to focus on innovation—creating the structure, the time, and the culture of innovation. When an employee enters an X-team program, he or she explicitly signs on to undertake an innovative project. Time is set aside for teams to brainstorm among themselves and with customers, experts, managers, and academics. Creativity is encouraged through exposure to stories of innovative teams and companies like Razr, the Netgen team, and IDEO. Checklists guide interactions with people inside and outside the firm and industry to benchmark best practices. Reporting to top-level managers, who ensure that the most innovative projects get praise and resources, enables high-quality projects that push into new terrain.

*Dilemma 2: Top managers have a vision, but how can they get the rest of the organization to implement the programs needed to realize it?*

We've all seen those PowerPoint presentations as the top management team lays out the vision and strategy for the firm. That is the easy part. More difficult is finding the talent to implement the strategy and figuring out how to translate the big idea into concrete projects and action. More difficult is creating broad understanding of the new directions throughout all levels of the firm. More difficult is gaining cooperation across different groups in the organization who have never worked together before. More difficult is getting the input of other levels within the firm so that local knowledge and insights can be incorporated into more global strategies. Enter X-teams.

X-team programs typically start with a big launch and end with project presentations. At both of these events, top managers are present. This is an opportunity for them to present their vision for what these projects might cover. While participants are not required to follow the dictates of top management, they often seek some guidelines about what problems and issues are most important to the top management team. This is just the start of the dialogue. Future interactions between participants and managers allow both groups to present ideas, get feedback, and work toward aligning their interests and passions. In this way top managers find teams that move their upper-level ideas into concrete projects and whose members are motivated and have reshaped the company's visions to align with current market and competitive conditions. With an X-team program, managers often get multiple solutions to their problems and multiple teams committed to change—so the impact is much larger than it would be with only one or two X-teams in place.

*Dilemma 3: Local line managers have ideas about what is not working in the firm and what customers want, but they feel powerless to make change happen.*

Our conversations with local line managers have shown us that of all the people in an organization, it is these managers who really have their hands on the pulse of the customer, the market, the local culture, and new trends in technology. They know which competitors are outbidding them and what customers are complaining about. They know this information firsthand but do not think that they can respond to it. Many would like to create new solutions for customers but feel that no one is listening or providing support for new ideas. They also feel pressed for time as it is, without taking on additional responsibilities. They often feel repressed by the organizational hierarchy, hemmed in by the rules and regulations within which organizations operate. All of this can lower morale within an organization, and if something is not done to stop it, the negativity spreads.

X-teams, then, become a vehicle of voice. At certain moments in an X-team program, participants are given their moment in the sun: they have the ear of top managers, and they can make their case. The rule in an X-team program is that no team should move ahead unless there is someone further up in the organizational hierarchy who supports its project. So the onus is on the team to sell its ideas. This usually isn't a problem: since team members are often quite passionate about their ideas, they appreciate even the opportunity to present their point of view and rally for their cause. They also often find that top managers provide input that helps fine-tune those ideas, show fatal flaws in members' reasoning, or transform ideas into ones that better fit new strategic directions and are more likely to garner support. It's important to note that the onus on top management is to listen; two-way communication must be ensured. This interaction across levels in the firm enables the information about customers, technologies, and markets to align with strategic initiatives.

*Dilemma 4: Leadership is centralized at the top, trying to solve problems alone, while the full power of the organization is underused in solving complex problems, implementing new solutions, and coordinating initiatives.*

The problems that plague today's world are difficult to solve—too difficult for a few people at the top of an organization to take on alone. Whether it's global warming or getting fuel-cell technology to see the light of day, poverty or civil war, or figuring out how to do business in a world of shifting political and economic realities, people in organizations will have to work together across boundaries to move ahead. The myth of the strong leader at the top who will solve all our troubles is just that— a myth. While it is certainly important to have strong top leadership, to apply the expertise and get-go needed for real change, many people need to be mobilized. Enter X-teams.

X-teams are the vehicle for distributed leadership. They are the mechanism by which many different people are harnessed to the task of understanding the problems we face, generating multiple solutions, building on prior knowledge, and then working with a host of others to get the wheels of change moving. It is the teams at Microsoft and BellCo, the Razr team at Motorola, Team Fox at Pharmaco, the Northwest team at the consulting organization, and the teams at BP and Merrill Lynch that have shown us a way to work at multiple levels of the firm to create new visions of what is possible and new ways to configure ourselves to make a difference. X-team programs can start this process.

So how does one create these X-teams? Five key factors are critical to implementing a formal program.

## Five Key Success Factors in Creating X-Teams

While all kinds of bells and whistles can go into an X-team program, five critical factors must be present for a program to fly: you must have commitment from the top, a solid launch, a stringent structure, support and feedback mechanisms, and a clear endgame.

### Success Factor 1: Commitment from the Top

Clearly, an X-team program won't succeed without strong commitment from the top management team. Management's active involvement not only provides legitimacy to the program and ensures the support of others in the organization; it also helps motivate participants and ensures that there is follow-up on the projects that the X-teams undertake. In short, top management sets the tone for the program and creates a culture of dialogue and distributed leadership.

The simple fact that the top management team is sponsoring an X-team program provides it with legitimacy. By saying even a few words at the launch, a manager signals to the rest of the organization that this activity is important. X-team members can then more easily contact others in the organization and expect a response. Once top management has decided which projects to support, it must then follow up and show its continued commitment.

The X-teams at both BP and Merrill Lynch have had staunch top management support. At BP two group vice presidents, Tony Meggs and Ellis Armstrong, have flown from London to Boston to spend time with all seven cadres while the Projects Academy classes are in session at MIT. Graham Cattell, director of projects, has engaged the Projects Academy to create Project Principles that change the way that project management is done at BP. The work of the Projects Academy has also won prestigious awards at BP and MIT. At Merrill Lynch, executive vice president Dow Kim—the primary sponsor of the program—attended all the sessions when the projects were reported out, decided to move ahead on many X-team projects, and asked his staff to track and report on their progress.

But it takes more than senior management presence, support, and resources to make an X-team program successful. Senior managers have to set up and reinforce a culture that will support X-teams: where managers encourage participants to talk to them, to describe what they care about and why they care about it. They must invite new ideas and perspectives and really listen to alternative views. X-teams only work if there is real two-way communication, and top management must be the role models that make this happen. All too often top managers will say they want to involve other parts of the organization, but new ideas are subsequently rejected. Managers fear giving control to others, and habitual routines (i.e., "this is how it's done here") are hard to break. Unless these patterns change, an X-team program will not succeed.

Building an X-team culture involves openness to spanning boundaries, sharing information, and challenging dogma at all levels of the organization. Top management can help build this culture by breaking down barriers, by fighting the "Not-Invented-Here" mentality, and by fostering a culture of sharing information, crossing boundaries, and nurturing innovation at lower levels of the firm. This is not easy and will take time, especially in very hierarchical and bureaucratic companies. An important building block is to train the troops in the language and behavior of X-teams. Whatever the vehicle for getting the word out, people in the organization need to know what X-teams are, what their building blocks and potential are, and how much top management values their work.

Despite top management's importance to X-teams, however, it's only part of the story. Equally critical is staffing X-teams with skilled members. People in the organization will take note of who is chosen to be in an X-team program, how their work is regarded, and what happens to them after the program is over. If being part of an X-team is seen as a good leadership development tool and a good career move, then it will attract the best people and they will try hard to be successful. Line managers will also get on board and support the program.

### Success Factor 2: A Solid Launch

Beginnings can hold the key to the way almost any endeavor unfolds, and this is never more true then when launching an X-team. At the launch, X-team members begin to identify and choose their projects, learn about what an X-team is and how to become one, and spend time together learning about other team members and preparing a plan for how they will work together. Particularly for geographically dispersed teams, this early meeting makes all the difference in getting a running start on the project and being able to stay connected throughout the process.

Imagine a large room with flip charts placed all around its perimeter. It is here that X-team members begin to identify the projects that they will work on. In some companies top management provides a complete list of the projects it wants to assign. In our experience the program is more successful if top managers offer some initial ideas of what projects they would like to see or leave the choice completely up to the team. We think that it is important to let X-teams find their own way—they should be invited to innovate, not told how they should do it or what solution they should come up with. Micromanagement of X-teams from the top runs counter to the whole nature and promise of the X-team and surely risks stifling the team's potential.

In some companies teams are preassigned, while in others they are left to form spontaneously based on the interests of individuals in the program. Some teams choose to be together based on geographic proximity, which makes meeting easier. Perhaps the most important aspect of project selection is that participants choose something to work on that they believe is really worthwhile. Projects are much more successful if members are motivated from the start, whether because they have personally had problems in a particular arena or because they think that they might be able to make a real difference.

Shared passion becomes the building block to finding others in the company who also share this view. The joint-venture team at BP wrote: "At our very first meeting . . . we recognized everyone in the team had great personal passion for the subject matter. This passion came from our individual belief that there was real value in getting our Joint Ventures right from the beginning. We had each experienced situations in the past where we hadn't gotten it right for a plethora of reasons. As we networked our 'problem statement' across our company, we found a very large number of equally passionate people with the very same thoughts and desires for change. This gives us comfort and confidence that with a little structure and process we can turn these shared passions into business results."

At BP topics are identified in consultation with project and business leaders. Each cohort of thirty people who go through the program discusses the issues and challenges identified. They are then free to choose their own projects and teams around areas of mutual interest. The teams receive guidance and mentoring from MIT and BP leaders. At Merrill Lynch teams are preassigned based on synergies of expertise or geographic proximity. Project ideas are kept very loose at this stage. The first thing that X-teams will be asked to do after leaving the launch session is to begin to explore an idea to see whether it is viable, to delve deeper to improve understanding of it, to learn how others have approached it in the past, and to discover how others view it now. Often projects change rather dramatically after everyone understands them more thoroughly.

Once a team has formed and chosen a preliminary project idea, then the transformation to becoming an X-team begins. The launch starts with a send-off from top management, and then the core ideas of effective X-teams are introduced through lectures, videotapes of effective teams in action, a presentation from former X-team members describing what they did, or a case that describes an X-team project in some depth. Follow-up readings are handed out. It is important that everyone in the program, from top management on down, shares the same language and concepts of X-teams so that people understand each other when they use words like *scouting* and *ambassadorship*, *visioning* and *inventing*, and *explore*, *exploit*, and *export*.

In many companies, X-teams are an integral part of an extensive learning and leadership development experience. For example, at BP participants are engaged in six residential weeks of courses at MIT, spread over the year of their X-team activity, during which they apply what they have learned from numerous faculty. At Merrill Lynch, X-team material is integrated with two faculty-led days and eighteen digital lectures on investment theory. In this way the X-team process gets paired with additional material that helps the team members to reinforce their learning and approach their project with added confidence and new expertise that can spur innovative ideas. But an X-team program need not be this involved—the five steps provide the basics.

After X-team members have had all their preliminary training, it is time to go to work. The more time that team members can spend getting to know each other and preparing for their early work of exploration, the higher the chance of hitting the ground running and succeeding. Here the checklists about setting the stage and the key tasks of exploration from the previous chapter are handed out, and team members are asked to meet together to get acquainted and to put together a work plan for the first month of their project. If time is not taken for this activity while members are together at the launch, then it is harder for team members to communicate, develop trust, and work together on the exploration task. This time also helps calm the anxiety inherent in the start of a team and provides a structure that allows members to see some immediate progress on their task. After this work is done, team members come back to a central room and present their plans to the other teams. Teams are encouraged to stay in touch during the course of the project and to try to help each other out while projects are going on.

### Success Factor 3: A Stringent Structure

The BP joint-venture team wrote almost comically about the "Magic of Milestones and the Delights of Discipline," but laying out for team members what they need to do and when they need to do it helps them direct their activities and make the best use of limited time and resources. Thus, the time and energy put into creating checklists containing step-by-step guidelines for getting started, exploration, exploitation, and exportation proves worthwhile. Add to that milestones, deliverables, and deadlines for each step along the road, and the X-team is on its way.

It is very helpful to have all the teams meet for the launch and again following exploration and for the final presentations. (Of course, these meetings are not possible when team projects are on different schedules.) Common meetings allow for what is known as "temporal crossing points," when everyone pauses at the same time.[2] Hence, projects can be evaluated simultaneously, members can shift teams if necessary, everyone is open to feedback and change since they are in pause mode, and shifts in the entire project structure can reflect the progress of all team projects.

The stringent structure begins with deadlines and deliverables for the end of the exploration, exploitation, and exportation phases of the project. By the end of exploration, team members must have engaged in sensemaking, trying to understand their project issues deeply and from multiple points of view. Using scouting, ambassadorship, and task coordination, they must collect data that is then put into a report of key findings and a plan for how they will shift to exploitation. During exploitation they must move from data collection to problem solving. The team needs to create a vision of how it can have the most impact in the company and then go about inventing ways to make that vision a reality. Again, scouting, ambassadorship, and task coordination must be used to create an innovative product, process, or idea, which gets put into a short presentation along with a plan for how to move to exportation. Finally, team members must follow the guidelines for exportation. Team members need to communicate their ideas and gain support from others in the organization who will take the project to the next stage—either implementing it throughout the organization or taking it to the marketplace, or committing additional resources for more work. This stage will have a deadline for a presentation to top management and a final report.

As the BP joint-venture team reported on its milestones and deadlines:

We all recognized that the Project Academy's guidelines looked a bit like a primary school workbook that might result in occasional rapped knuckles. It has only been in retrospect that we have seen that there is real creative power in clearly writing down instructions, giving context, defining milestone deliverables and giving hard-edged time deadlines of delivery for everyone on the team to use and rally around. This process . . . made sure we really did take the time to dig deeply into our subject, test drive a lot of different tools and approaches and broaden our network of input and influence. In order to deliver these "learning" milestones we decided early on that we would hold a weekly conference telephone call at GMT + 1 [Greenwich Mean Time plus one hour] known as "Come Hell or High Water." The discipline of this meeting kept the flywheel spinning from our original meeting to the submission of this report.

### *Success Factor 4: Support and Feedback Mechanisms*

While the magic of milestones and the delights of discipline provide the basic framework from which team members work, they often need support and feedback along the way. Teams need sponsorship whereby someone from the company is evaluating their project deliverables and letting them know whether they are on the right track. This allows the team to redirect, or make its case again, to ensure a high-quality outcome. Sponsors can also check on the process of the team to make sure that internal dynamics as well as external activity and action are going well. Sponsors should be within the managerial ranks and should explicitly play a coaching as well as evaluating role. They can be assisted by technical experts, if more content feedback is needed, and by facilitators, if process consultation is needed to help the team work effectively.

Periodic check-ins before major deliverables are due help the team stay on track and identify problems before they get out of hand. During check-ins team members are encouraged to talk about what is working and what is not. Frequent problems include distributing the workload unequally, finding the time to work on the project given heavy workloads or vacations, having difficulty getting in touch with people outside the team, or discovering that what the team wanted to do is not feasible. Teams may need help working on how to distribute work across members, making sure that the project scope is feasible, gaining access to others, or starting over with a new idea.

Both BP and Merrill Lynch provided a lot of support and feedback to the teams. The managers who work on these programs are often the glue that holds them together. These are the people who are the real heroes of these programs (e.g., Peter Duff, Judy Wagner, and Jim Breson from BP, and Kathleen Goldreich at Merrill Lynch), making sure that everything gets organized (from schedules and materials to executive sessions), coaching members, linking the teams to the rest of the organization and top management ranks, and facilitating the teams' activities. Staff from inside the company are paired with experts outside the company to create coaching teams. The coaching teams work very hard to make sure that X-teams have sponsorship and are getting the resources and help they need. Internal staff provide contacts within the firm, while outside experts facilitate process problems or comment on the teams' ideas. Check-ins are often done by phone, given the global composition of the teams.

In the absence of (or in addition to) coaching teams, a set of X-teams can be given a mentor. One thing an organization can do is to recognize and reward experienced people for spending time sharing expertise and know-how with teams that lack experience of their own. We have come across a number of such systems of designated experts. At Ford, for instance, "wise men" who have deep and broad experience with developing new cars and have many contacts throughout the company are rewarded for sharing their wisdom with teams that need it. More important, the time wise men spend on others' projects is explicitly recognized.[3]

Support can also come in the form of an effective information system. This is particularly important for X-teams operating in a context of widely dispersed and changing knowledge. Such a system may include databases that give access to critical know-how, but just as important, it may also include "know-who" databases and expert-finding systems. These databases can point team members in the direction of who has done something before. But information systems can also include access to Web sites, blogs, and other communication vehicles that enable team members, as well as members of multiple teams, to share information and solve problems together. Having access to a wide range of talent and expertise is part of how an X-team works, and an effective information system can support this activity.

### Success Factor 5: A Clear Endgame

The last critical success factor is managing the ending of the teams. Here top managers need to listen to the project results and recommendations, praise the X-team members for the work they have done, decide which projects will move forward and which will not, and begin to ensure that whatever follow-up activities need to take place are assigned to the appropriate manager. The final presentations are an opportunity for X-team members to have the visibility and voice that they were promised. For those who get to move ahead, future assignments may be forthcoming. For those whose projects are not going to be ramped up, rationale for the choice needs to be explained. The decision not to go ahead with a project should be celebrated as much as the decision to go forward if the team has done a good job. In any case, the final reports are an opportunity for celebration since everyone has learned a great deal and all have many more skills, more experiences, and greater understanding than they did before. Often the day ends with a celebratory dinner to reward all team members and managers.

But while the project presentations mark an ending to the actual projects, there is still a lot of work to be done. For top management this is only the beginning. These managers need to show that they have listened, and they need to make sure that the necessary follow-up is done. For the Merrill Lynch team, Dow Kim assigned a manager to the new distressed equity desk realizing the need to protect this experiment in a cross-unit venture. For the Microsoft team, Bill Gates took half the Netgen team away to start a new unit that would make its learnings a normal part of Microsoft's business practices. Whatever is needed, top managers have to ensure that all the X-teams' hard work is put to good use.

For team members, there is usually pressure to move on to the next task and the next project. But if there is constant movement and activity, learning can suffer. Without strong norms and incentives dictating the importance of learning from recently completed projects, it is unlikely that time will be spent on this activity. Key here is giving teams the time to assemble lessons learned and to think about what they want to carry forward to their next team assignments. Key here is also writing reports—not multi-inch project reviews that no one will ever read, but short lesson documents. These might include the ten things that an X-team should never do and the ten things that an X-team must always do. This might include a list of the most helpful people to the team and leads that took the team down blind alleys. Important, too, are success stories. Once one or two stories that embody the spirit, activities, and outcomes of successful X-teams are out there, they should be broadcast widely. This is the surest way for time-pressured team members to take note and for culture change to begin.

The X-team programs illustrated in this chapter create a kind of infrastructure of innovation within companies. They pull team members out of their everyday jobs and mind-sets and challenge them to move from passion to action—through new products and new ways to improve key business processes—and then to make their innovative ideas part of ongoing organizational practice. In effect, companies like BP and Merrill

Lynch have created X-teams to lead their organizations in new directions and to improve their one piece of the world. And more and more companies are joining their ranks. CVRD, a Brazilian mining company, and News Corporation have created X-team programs also in the context of their executive education programs to improve the process of going global and better leveraging IT talent, respectively.

This chapter has outlined how an organization can take concrete steps to launch an organization-wide X-team program. For such a program to take root, however, the organization needs to have a structure in place that provides a fertile soil for distributed leadership through X-teams. The steps top management can take to create a supportive context is the topic of our concluding chapter.

# NINE

# X-Teams

## *Distributed Leadership in Action*

E ARLY IN ITS HISTORY Southwest Airlines was in big trouble.[1] The larger carriers like Braniff and Texas International
decided that they had to do something about the competitive threat
coming from Southwest. So they undercut prices along Texas routes.
While Southwest's top management was appealing to loyal customers to
pay the extra money to stay with the airline, more radical change was
needed. To make payroll, Southwest had just sold one of its four planes.
Now the airline faced a huge dilemma. How could it transport the same
number of passengers with three planes as it had with four? Solving this
dilemma would mean the difference between survival and bankruptcy.
And the CEO alone could not come up with a viable solution.

So the whole company was put to work. Enter an X-team made up of
baggage handlers and ground crew, flight attendants and even pilots. With
input from airport workers and regulators, they brainstormed lots of ideas.
Based on their knowledge of the work that had to be done to turn a plane
around—a process that includes landing, getting passengers off the plane,

cleaning it, getting food and fuel on board, loading passengers, and taking off again—they invented a new way of organizing themselves. In this new mode of operating, they cut their turnaround time from the industry average of forty-five to sixty minutes down to ten. While turnaround time at Southwest has since increased due to its use of larger planes and to new FAA procedures, the other major airlines have yet to catch up. And Southwest has gone on to become one of the most successful airlines in the industry. The company excels at employee development and involvement, but it has also remained profitable for thirty years running, even through 9/11 and the oil crises and high costs that have plagued the industry.

Southwest constantly involves employees in problem solving and innovation, giving them a lot of leeway in deciding what needs to be done to make sure that customers have a positive experience and operations run smoothly. There is a lot of contact across levels of the firm and rewards and recognition for people who make a difference. Furthermore, the leaders at the top create conditions that enable others in the organization to take charge. Top management establishes the core values, like customer service and integrity, and then lets employees figure out how best to bring those values to life. All of this makes Southwest Airlines a veritable poster child for distributed leadership.

## Leadership at All Levels

Distributed leadership assumes that the more organizations disperse leadership throughout their structure, the more effective they are. This does not mean that executive leadership is unimportant; certainly if there is not effective leadership at the top, then the organization will not function well. But effective executive leadership alone isn't sufficient for organizational success. In our model, leadership must exist at all levels of the firm, and anyone who feels as if he or she can make a contribution is able to take on a leadership role.

For example, at Oxfam there are at least three levels of leadership. There is executive leadership at the top of the organization, led by Barbara Stocking, the director general of Oxfam, UK. The managers at this level determine the overall strategy for the organization and the focus that Oxfam will take. Like other nongovernment organizations (NGOs), Oxfam cannot take on all the problems of the people it serves. The system works better if NGOs allocate their resources to specific issues, like poverty, AIDS, hunger, or education. But an overall strategy crafted in London, even with the input of people from around the world, must be customized to the needs of specific countries and cultures. Enter the country managers. Their job is to follow directives from on high and also to shape those directives so that they work for the particular country's political and cultural climate and for the specific needs of the people in that region. Stocking and her team spend a lot of time with the country managers so they're clear on how a centralized scope, focus, and structure can work hand in hand with the specific needs of different regions. Country managers then work with local NGOs, government, and the private sector to link their programs to a more general Oxfam strategy.

Then there are the employees who are on the ground doing the organization's work with the people in cities and small villages. These employees tend to be highly motivated to help others achieve their rights. But again, they must have a focus, and that comes from the top, with input from all levels. However, if there is a crisis, or no one else is available to give other kinds of care, then the Oxfam people on the scene need to have the leeway to move outside their sphere of work to deal with the issue at hand, such as the tsunami response. The shifting demands on the ground create conditions ripe for X-teams, made up of people from within Oxfam and often other NGOs, to bring care where it is most needed and to link to the programs created by the country managers.

Increasingly, companies practicing distributed leadership are involving not just people within their own boundaries but many outside as well to improve operations, create innovative new products, and solve complex problems. Distributed leadership is used to help turn companies around and bring a wider pool of expertise to the problem-solving and decision-making process. While the myth of the one great leader at the top is still alive and well in many people's minds, those who are able to picture this one leader surrounded and supported by many others throughout the organization are the ones moving ahead. Another example is Procter & Gamble.

When A. G. Lafley was appointed CEO of Procter & Gamble (P&G) in 1999, the proud firm was adrift.[2] A champion of consumer products brands, the giant Cincinnati-based company had experienced a long drought of new products. Revenues and earnings were slipping badly. Five years later, however, the firm was once again the innovation leader of the industry. After a string of hits, sales for fiscal 2004 were up almost 20 percent and earnings improved 25 percent—a remarkable feat for a firm of P&G's size.

Behind the turnaround lies a strategic two-step bet. First, Lafley staked the firm's future growth on innovation. Second, he launched an innovation strategy that built on established brands, thus leveraging core P&G assets. Adding single-serving packages and chips with trivia questions increased Pringles' market share almost 15 percent. The old Mr. Clean brand was extended with a record-selling line of car-washing products. Similarly, the Crest line was pushed into whitening products. Whitestrips and Night Effects gel have helped double Crest's revenue in just four years—to $2 billion. On Lafley's watch, the number of P&G brands selling more than a billion dollars a year has rocketed from ten to sixteen.

As anyone trying to thrive in innovation-based competition knows, launching a strategy based on innovation is easy to say but very difficult to do. Why? The actual innovation can't be implemented from the executive suite. So how has P&G done it? The road to this spurt of innovation has been paved with distributed leadership, bringing new product ideas to the company from the front lines of the global marketplace. It used to be that all new products came from central R&D. Now they originate in many places, both inside and outside the organization. Swiffer Duster and Mr. Clean Magic Eraser are two products whose seeds came from discoveries outside P&G. In fact, 35 percent of new products now come from the outside. Lafley has said that he wants to increase that to 50 percent. When asked why, he said, "It's just a number I made up. For me it's just a metaphor for the fact that we don't care where the ideas come from."[3]

Driving distributed leadership at P&G is a model of innovation that the firm refers to as "connect and develop," or C&D, rather than R&D.[4] The idea is to connect with opportunities in the firm's far-flung network and then to develop these seeds into fully fledged products based on P&G's considerable product development and marketing capabilities. What makes the external connection and the subsequent technology transfer work? X-teams.

Consider the wildly successful line of Pringles potato chips with trivia questions printed right on the chips, launched in 2004. The idea came up in a Pringles team brainstorming session. Everyone on the team agreed that it was a great idea. But how could it be done? It turned out that this simple idea required a sophisticated technological solution—a solution that P&G didn't have. In the old days, this would have triggered a long internal R&D effort. Instead, the team went into scouting mode. It defined a "technology brief," describing what was required, and circulated it in the firm's network in search of a solution. That is how a bakery in Bologna, Italy, was discovered as having invented a method for printing images on cookies. The technology was transferred back to Cincinnati and adapted for use by the Pringles team in record time.

## The Four Core Capabilities of Distributed Leadership

Companies like P&G, Oxfam, and Southwest all exhibit four capabilities, which we first discussed in chapter 5, that make them masters of distributed leadership: sensemaking, relating, visioning, and inventing. In a distributed leadership model, these capabilities are spread across individuals, units, and levels of the firm to tap the intellectual, interpersonal, rational, intuitive, conceptual, and creative capacities needed in today's organizations. This model views each specific leader as "incomplete"—that is, in need of working with others throughout the organization, wherever "expertise, vision, new ideas, and commitment are to be found."[5] To reiterate, these capabilities include:

- **Sensemaking.** The first core leadership capability, what Karl Weick refers to as "sensemaking," involves making sense of the context in which the organization is operating—being the eyes that read the opportunities and threats of a changing environment.[6] Clearly, dialogue and frequent communication up and down the organization is key to understanding the organizational terrain, as is communication to outside stakeholders and sources of expertise and new ideas. Connecting to what's out there and mapping customer demands, cultural norms, competitive challenges, technological advances, and market opportunities is essential to really understanding the current environment. This communication with external constituencies requires multiple networks to access new ideas, trends, and associations that can lead to new combinations and meshing needs with solutions. These external connections are as important at the CEO level as they are for the bench scientist, the marketer, and the engineer.

- **Relating.** This involves developing key relationships within and across organizations and bringing commitment and energy to the task. Trust is central. Frank communication won't work without trust. Team members at Southwest Airlines, Oxfam, and P&G would not search for new solutions and new ways of working together if they thought that top management was only trying to outsource their jobs. Similarly, executives need to trust

the corporate entrepreneurs and mavericks at the front lines
to exercise leadership, even if those frontline employees are
implementing things differently than the executives themselves
would do. Add to trust the essential dialogue that is needed
both to understand divergent views and opinions and to advo-
cate what each leader thinks is important, and you have effective relating.

- **Visioning.** This is about creating a compelling picture of the future. While sensemaking is all about "what is," visioning is about
  "what is possible" in the future. But visioning is more than the vision statement that companies post; it is a process of articulating
  what members of an organization may be able to create in the future. To work, that vision needs to be clear, well communicated,
  and able to define the parameters of action. A clear and well-
  communicated vision conveys the values, priorities, and direction
  within which frontline leaders have the freedom to act. Some
  leaders also push the frontiers of these boundaries. When Jim
  Parker was CEO at Southwest, there were always revenue targets
  and performance goals, but it was also clear that the customer
  came first, that people learned from their mistakes, and that
  learning—not blame—was the key to creating the kind of organization employees wanted to join. Others in the organization provided creative new ways to serve the customer and pushed the
  vision in new directions. For Barbara Stocking, Oxfam's role in
  the world is to work interdependently with people in need and to
  provide them with the tools to improve their lives, not to create
  dependency and greater poverty. This vision is continuously
  shaped by interaction with country managers and people on the
  ground. P&G's A. G. Lafley had a vision making it clear that new
  ideas were at a premium, that where they came from did not matter, and that the company's future was staked on innovation. It's

important to note that at P&G, C&D is not about outsourcing innovation. It is about finding ideas outside, as well as inside, and then actually implementing those ideas by building on the firm's core strengths. As expressed by Larry Huston and Nabil Sakkab, innovation executives at P&G, the vision is about having half of the innovation coming *from* the firm's own labs and the other half *through* them.[7]

- **Inventing.** The final leadership capability is about coming up with innovative solutions and designing new ways of working together to realize the vision. Inventing involves developing creative ways to get around roadblocks and keeping the organization moving as it shifts in new directions. The team at Southwest Airlines described at the start of this chapter invented a new way to turn planes around that has provided competitive advantage ever since. Oxfam employees are always inventing new ways to deal with harsh and changing local conditions, while Barbara Stocking is inventing at the corporate level. P&G's Lafley has set the parameters of innovation and in so doing has energized hundreds of employees to invent new ideas for tired brands.

It's important to understand that these four capabilities are not the sole responsibility of the CEO; they are shared. The key role of relating to the customer at Southwest occurs not through the CEO but through frontline employees who have direct access with the ticketing and servicing of those customers. For example, in the days after 9/11, Southwest employees rounded up passengers stranded at one airport and took them out for dinner and bowling. In another case, a Southwest employee saved a customer's baggage from being thrown away (belonging to an indigent passenger, the baggage was mistaken for trash because she had covered it in newspaper to protect it). These are the kinds of leadership acts that breed customer loyalty. Similarly, the country managers at Oxfam must constantly engage in sensemaking to ensure that local conditions are monitored and needs met. P&G employees are busy refining Lafley's vision and putting their own spin on future possibilities.

## X-Teams and Distributed Leadership

Throughout this book we have made the argument that X-teams are the vehicle by which distributed leadership takes place. Weaving these various arguments together shows that X-teams can help an organization spread leadership across the firm and embody the four capabilities in multiple ways:

- **Scouting.** This activity brings fresh ideas into the organization and encourages people to see the world through new eyes. Scouting helps create an up-to-date map of the world as it is right now, so that the organization can engage in sensemaking and then can adapt as needed.

- **Ambassadorship.** Ambassadorship links upper and lower levels of the firm, and it helps upper management find unique ways to solve complex problems and innovate and to give structure and body to new strategic initiatives. It enables people at lower levels of the firm to use their knowledge of customers, cultures, technologies, competitors, and markets to influence strategy and gives voice to those employees throughout the firm. Ambassadorship also allows multiple layers of the firm to align visioning and inventing, while creating relationships up and down the organization.

- **Task coordination.** This activity enables the firm to learn and coordinate across units, breaking down silos and inventing new synergies across units. It pushes new teams to build on the work of previous ones and to provide new strategic solutions based on efficiencies within the organization. Moreover, task coordination fosters relationships across disparate parts of the organization, as well as with people or companies outside.

- **Extreme execution.** Extreme execution helps provide the organization with a climate and culture of trust and open communication, thus facilitating relating. It also enables a sense of solidarity and safety necessary for innovation. Finally, extreme execution provides the organization with efficient and effective problem solving and implementation, facilitating inventing while sowing the seeds of a distributed leadership culture.

- **Explore-exploit-export.** This three-phrase approach provides a template to help X-team members sequence their core tasks of sensemaking, visioning, relating, and inventing because it sets them up to shift their focus over time and move from observation and understanding to action. After mapping the world, members create a vision of what they want to create and then move to making their dreams a reality. Finally, explore-exploit-export helps ensure that the work of the team transitions into the broader organization if that move is appropriate.

- **X-factors.** X-factors help the team to forge dense networks of contacts inside and outside the firm, creating the raw material for innovation and success through internal and external relationships. Notably, the fluid structure of expandable tiers facilitates adaptation and puts just the right number and type of people together to accomplish the task at hand and invent new ways of working together. The tiers distribute the varied tasks of leadership to different individuals and enable people to lead in some situations and take a more operational or advisory role in others.

All of this is to say that X-teams pull people out of their everyday jobs and provide them with a broader view of the firm so that they too can fully comprehend the complexity of making change happen and do their part. X-teams provide the organization with the ability to experiment with new procedures and initiatives to see what works and what does not. X-teams demonstrate distributed leadership in action in that teams engage in sensemaking, relating, visioning, and inventing. They also encourage leadership below the top level of the firm while enabling alignment of leadership activities up and down the hierarchy and across organizational boundaries. All the X-teams cited in this book illustrate how this process operates.

Recall, for example, the Northwest consulting team featured in chapter 1. The president of the consulting organization faced dissatisfied clients: the school districts his organization was supposed to serve. For one thing, the districts wanted more comprehensive initiatives with integrated solutions. So the president created teams with people from multiple functions, and he asked them to service multiple needs in the districts. The teams that succeeded did so because they explored before they acted. They spent a lot of time within their districts and tried to understand the districts' needs, not through their old lenses as functional specialists, but with their new lenses as problem solvers—as leaders. They engaged in active sensemaking and created deeper relationships with core stakeholders. Then they tried a variety of ways to serve this customer and learned from their mistakes and from feedback. This process led to innovative new practices like a new school evaluation process. These teams engaged in inventing. With ambassadorship, the top teams, like the Northwest team, were able to share these new practices with the president, and he, in turn, spread them to other teams. And so X-teams provided multiple experiments about how to approach a new and complex challenge for the organization, and several of them turned out to be the answer to better serving customer needs. These teams actually helped craft the vision of the whole company.

At BellCo a new organizational design was put together at corporate headquarters to enable the firm to offer its customers systems solutions with industry specialization. This new design required more integration across sales, technical services, installation, repair, and other organizational functions but did not specify exactly how this integration would happen. The Big Bank team helped flesh out this vision and invented a way to make it a reality. The Big Bank teammates took the lead in figuring out the needs of their industry. They then took the lead in figuring out exactly what systems selling would entail (sensemaking) and then forged links with other parts of the organization to make it happen (relating). They were entrepreneurial, they learned, and they gave detail, breadth, and definition to the new design (inventing). They were as much the leaders of this change as the top managers who had created the original design and vision.

Other teams cited in this book—teams like Netgen, Fox, and Razr—showed that same level of distributed leadership in action when carrying out their tasks. And it made all the difference to their success—and the success of their organizations.

## The Role of Top Management: Crafting a Culture for X-Teams

We have seen how X-teams, by the force of their structure, process, and success, can change the culture of organizations to be more entrepreneurial and more innovative. They can also be the engine of distributed leadership as they take on the tasks of sensemaking, relating, visioning, and inventing and spread these leadership tasks throughout the organization. Top management, however, can help speed up the process by creating a cultural context that is a fertile ground for distributed leadership and innovation in general, and for X-teams in particular.

Here we explore how top management can craft an X-team culture. But make no mistake: crafting a culture takes time and energy; change will not be evident overnight. The concept of organizational culture can be quite elusive. We've found a simple model first introduced by our colleague Ed Schein very useful in this context.[8] According to Schein, culture exists at three levels. First, culture includes visible artifacts that are manifested in management activities, incentive systems, and organizational structures. They are also seen in more subtle things, such as office design, dress code, and language. Second, there are the stated values about why the organization exists, such as serving customer needs or improving shareholder value, and how leadership in the organization should be exerted, such as through top-down leadership or through distributed leadership. These stated values are what is often found in the official mission statements so popular with many organizations. But culture includes a third element: underlying basic assumptions. Much of what is important about culture exists at this level, and we can't see it directly. There are tacit rules about how to get things done, beliefs about what's right and what's wrong, what's fair and what's not. These kinds of deeply held assumptions are what mostly drive culture and behavior, and when we talk about culture change, this is the level of culture we're referring to. After all, we not only want to change what people do, how they dress, or what they say, but we want to change their whole mind-set.

Unfortunately, just as we can't see these basic assumptions directly, we can't change them directly. The trick is to communicate the stated values consistently and at every opportunity, and to manage the artifacts so that they are aligned with these values—so that over time, the basic assumptions we'd like the organization to embody take hold. We've already discussed in chapter 8 the need for top management to communicate the values of distributed leadership and to get the word out about X-teams, what they are, the promise that they bring to the organization, and so on. Now we highlight six management activities (artifacts in Schein's terminology) that can help reinforce the stated values and shape the basic assumptions of a culture in which X-teams can thrive.

### *Activity 1: Provide Strategic Direction*

A company's strategy is the engine that drives the actions of distributed leadership and X-teams. Without it, leadership at the front lines would be directionless and ineffective. For example, at P&G management directs its X-teams in three ways. First, it gears scouting toward the top ten consumer needs—a list that is reassessed by top management yearly. The needs are then broken down into scientific problems to be solved and spelled out in technology briefs (as described in the Pringles team example earlier in this chapter). Second, so-called adjacencies (new products that build on existing brand assets) are identified. For example, tooth-whitening products are adjacencies to the Crest brand; they go beyond toothpaste. Finally, management uses "technology game boards" to identify possible bridges between a technology and multiple brands. This is a way to investigate whether a potential external technology acquisition can help more than one family of products.

At BP management creates teams to provide new ways to manage major projects. While teams are free to choose their own projects, top managers offer input by identifying areas as particularly important for project management. At CVRD, the Brazilian mining company, the focus of X-teams is on going global. Management regularly pushes people beyond their day-to-day jobs and pairs them with people from other areas of the company to stimulate creative new ways to help CVRD innovate as it moves outside Brazil in businesses identified as strategically critical. In short, the task of top management is to create the strategic direction, or umbrella, under which other levels of leadership can fall.

### *Activity 2: Manage Overload and Empower People*

Being a frontline leader and the member of an X-team can be an exhilarating and empowering experience. But it also risks adding to what is often an already heavy workload. In chapter 8 we argued that X-teams can help solve the dilemma of creating competitive advantage through innovation while at the same time doing the day-to-day work of an efficiency-driven, hard-charging organization. This will not work, however, if being charged with spearheading an X-team is just added to the existing workload.

Overload is a chronic problem in today's organizations. It is often exacerbated by a misguided macho attitude that "good" managers can handle stretch goals. A high-potential individual, thus, is supposed to be able to juggle more and more projects. This logic is very dangerous, particularly when it involves strategically important innovation projects. Overloaded team members are not likely to think creatively and come up with fresh ideas and breakthrough innovation. In fact, a key role of top management is to make sure that this does not happen. If top management does not protect would-be frontline leaders from overload, they run a very high risk of failing and creating cynicism and burnout instead of a culture for X-teams to thrive in.[9]

To manage overload top-level managers must give people time off to do innovative projects. They can also provide resources in the form of executive education courses, travel money for distributed teams, and support—secretarial, coaching, financial, and systems—to help X-teams do the work they need to do. Extra vacation time or family time is helpful following X-team programs, particularly if these programs have involved extensive travel and study abroad.

Related to the theme of overload is the theme of empowerment. While top management often encourages lower-level employees to experiment and come up with new ideas, this behavior might put those employees in conflict with middle management, managers of other units, or the top managers themselves. Furthermore, top-level management may be simultaneously encouraging innovation while pushing lower levels to tougher and tougher performance and economic targets. Add the cultural expectation of operating according to rules, and pressure builds. Lower-level managers need to be given the equivalent of a flare—something to signal that the demands are too high. A flare might be sent up if targets mean working people or machinery beyond what is safe or healthy or if the only way to succeed is to cut corners that undermine the culture of quality.

More important, sending a flare needs to be read and treated as a positive thing, not as an act requiring punishment. Beyond flares, lower-level leaders need to be protected so that they have the freedom to communicate bad news or excess pressure that puts individuals and organizations at risk. Ombudsmen, anonymous electronic bulletin boards, and open-door policies provide people with venues in which they can communicate problems without fear of retribution.

### Activity 3: Be Ambidextrous

Recent research has shown that firms with so-called ambidextrous senior teams have more success in managing sustained innovation.[10] An ambidextrous person can use both her left and right hands, and an ambidextrous senior team can manage both the mature parts of the business requiring coordination and control *and* the innovation-driven part of the business requiring entrepreneurship and freedom from the old ways. Such a senior team is likely to do much better at supporting distributed leadership and X-teams. So what is it that an ambidextrous senior team should be able to do? It starts with a recognition that running the established business and creating innovative ideas demand different skills and different ways of thinking and that they are often at odds. It is not that one way is better than the other; it is that they are different and good for different things. Both are necessary for the long-term success of innovation-driven businesses. Specifically, being ambidextrous means being able to manage divergent incentive systems and to allocate resources to allow for different time horizons, rates of return, and milestones.

The context put in place for the Razr team is a case in point. The performance metrics and the sales forecasts were different from—and much lower than—other more traditional product development projects at Motorola. This reflected the higher level of risk involved and higher levels of uncertainty. In addition, the team was protected from ongoing oversight and interference from middle management. Team members needed the safety and freedom to experiment with new ideas and fail, without being told that they were breaking rules or not meeting traditional revenue targets. It turned out that Razr exceeded even the most optimistic scenarios. But had the team been forced to follow the same road map as product development teams in more established businesses—with time tracking, early pressure for impressive ROI numbers, and so forth—chances are it would not have had the leeway to take the unorthodox paths that eventually led to the happy ending. A team cannot put this context in place by itself. Only ambidextrous top management, which understands the unique needs of different kinds of teams, can.

### Activity 4: Promote Networks

Radical innovation is increasingly done in small and midsized entrepreneurial firms that tend to view technologies and markets differently, with fresh eyes and ideas. Even many individual inventors have great new ideas that they are eager to license. Add to that the increasing numbers of universities forming industry alliances and making money from their research. All of these developments, of course, have been accelerated by the Internet, enabling connections that would earlier have been impossible or, at least, highly unlikely. This new ecology constitutes a web of innovation opportunities. Some have referred to it as a new paradigm of "open innovation."[11] X-teams are supremely placed as vehicles to capitalize on the opportunities offered by this era of open innovation. Top management can help by promoting the building of networks through which those opportunities flow.

Consider the case of P&G, which is purposefully and continuously building many networks of different kinds. For example, the company builds proprietary networks such as one consisting of more than seventy technology entrepreneurs around the world who are employed by P&G and whose job is to scout for opportunities (such as meeting with university researchers) and to develop supplier contacts. But the company is also nurturing open networks such as yet2.com, a Web site for the exchange of intellectual property funded by a large group of *Fortune* 100 companies. Both kinds of networks create tremendous value and exciting opportunities for P&G's X-teams.

There are many other ways to promote networks both inside and outside the firm. Within the firm it has now become commonplace to send whole teams or units, rather than individuals, to quality- or executive-training sessions. In this way strong, deep ties are created within a company. Corporatewide events that mix people from different levels and parts of an organization put people together who would not ordinarily meet. Finally, the creation of Tiger teams—teams that are given assignments for core tasks like planning, budgeting, or project oversight—put people in cross-unit teams that create horizontal connections across the company.

External networks can be supported by encouraging and funding employees to go to conferences, trade shows, and industry events of all kinds. Customer meetings that provide feedback on products also serve to link customers to each other and to sales, marketing, and even the engineers who will design the next generation of products.

Some companies are even sponsoring executive programs for their customers, not to do a hard sell, but simply to deepen the relationships across firm boundaries.

### Activity 5: Practice Temporal Leadership

What, you might ask, is temporal leadership? This is the idea that top-level leaders can use time, and temporal change, to facilitate X-team behavior. Imagine the difficulties inherent in managing an X-team. Members have to align to top management, which operates on a fiscal calendar; middle management, which operates on budgeting and planning cycles; other functional groups, each with its own time frame for operating; and customer deadlines. Add to this the fact that X-teams may need to shift resources, people, and ideas from one team to another, a process made more difficult when teams are operating on different schedules. If this were an orchestra, with each group representing a different instrument, it would produce a cacophony of sounds as each instrument followed its own score.

Now consider a temporal redesign. Suppose all X-teams were on the same schedule, launched simultaneously, and working toward common deadlines. Each interim deadline then becomes a common stopping point and "temporal crossing point" during which teams can be evaluated simultaneously.[12] Then comparisons become easier because all teams are at the same stage of development. Furthermore, as decisions are made to shift people and resources around, teams are open to changes since they have all paused—finished with one mode of work and ready to shift into another. This intervention is even stronger if the stopping point corresponds to key shifts in the task, such as the movement to exploitation and exportation.

Let's take the temporal design one step further. Create an organizational rhythm whereby all groups within a unit or across several units need to work to the same milestones and deadlines. Now there is one common score. This might mean getting a new product out at the same time every year or breaking the day in half, with morning time reserved for interruptions and joint work while afternoons are reserved for individual concentration.[13] Or this might mean that all groups must get code in by 3 p.m. for joint testing of the prototype or that a hospital schedule centers on patient needs, not clinical services schedules. Consider a contest within a unit for new ideas for soft drinks. The contest is timed for the fall so that winning ideas can be chosen in winter and turned into possible new product candidates by late spring—just in time for testing during the annual customer meeting. The flow of work is scheduled in these instances to mesh with key internal and external deadlines. Then all organizational groups need to pace their work accordingly.

By setting up such rhythms and cycles, the cacophony of sounds turns into a real musical composition. Different parts of the organization know when they have to coordinate their efforts with others to get the work done on time. In this scenario it is easier for X-teams to mesh their activities with other X-teams and other parts of the organization, as well as with the deadlines set by key external stakeholders. Now everyone basically shares the same pause, reflection, and shift to a new form of work.

### Activity 6: Be Role Models

No matter what structures and processes are put in place, one of the major spectator sports in organizations is watching top-level leaders. Their behavior is obsessively observed and analyzed to determine the signals they're sending out about what's important, how things are done around here, and what's really rewarded. Thus, top-level leaders need to pay close attention to what signals they are sending.

Schein points out several mechanisms by which leaders send signals.[14] The first is through their calendars—how they spend their time. If members of an X-team program are told that they have to link up the organizational hierarchy to engage in ambassadorship but then those up above never have time to meet, these team members will understand that there is no real commitment to the program. Similarly, if innovation is touted as a top priority but no time is spent on innovative projects, then no innovation will result. On the other hand, when senior managers from BP fly to another continent to attend the launch and final presentations of each X-team cadre, they are signaling that these projects are important to them and to the company.

Second, signals are sent through promotions, measurement systems, and resource allocation. Who is it that gets the next plum job? If top-level leaders are talking about innovation but only those managers who have great financial results are promoted, then the message will get out to play it safe and make your numbers—innovation is just too risky. On the other hand, if integrity is a core value and a manager who gets great results through questionable practices is passed over for promotion, word will spread that the top group is serious. At the same time, you can't encourage innovation and integrity without measuring them. If they are not measured, they are often ignored, and it is harder to make promotions in the absence of data. In the same vein, resource allocation decisions signal what the organization's priorities are. At Southwest Airlines there is a stated value that leadership at all levels is important. This value is supported and signaled by the fact that supervisory training for first-level supervisors has never been cut, even when the airline was facing fierce economic pressures.

Finally, signals are sent through stories. Top-level leaders can signal changes in a culture by telling stories that highlight new role models or behaviors. The story about the team that saved Southwest from bankruptcy early in its history is told over and over again to signal that all members of the organization are valued because they are core contributors to the company. Similarly, the story about the heroic deeds of the employee who saved some baggage from the garbage is told over and over again to point out that every customer is important. The key idea is that stories of great leadership throughout the firm will encourage distributed leadership in a way that self-promotion at the top simply will not accomplish.

In sum, top-level leaders communicate the values and vision of distributed leadership and X-teams, provide overall strategic direction, empower lower-level employees, promote networks, practice temporal leadership, and act as role models. They are more likely than other leaders to see the basic assumptions of distributed leadership take hold in their organization, as well as the successful implementation of X-teams.

## X-Teams: A Challenging Choice—with Great Rewards

Consider Thomas Friedman's words: "[W]hile the globalizing force in Globalization 1.0 was countries globalizing and the dynamic force in Globalization 2.0 was companies globalizing, the dynamic force in Globalization 3.0 . . . is small groups globalizing."[15] Throughout this book we have argued that X-teams are a particularly valuable tool for distributed leadership in today's global and innovation-driven world. But they are not for every situation. Their very nature as tools for leading change makes them hard to manage. X-teams are a challenging choice: coordination in an X-team is considerably more complicated than in a traditional team and can be taxing for team members. Before taking on the challenge, therefore, managers have to think hard about whether it is worth it for their organization. If the need for innovation, flexibility, and coordination is not clear, then a traditional team may be a better solution.

That cautionary note notwithstanding, we believe that modern society is moving in a direction in which more organizations will be gravitating toward the X-team model. While in this book we have mostly discussed examples of teams in competition-driven businesses, the forces of change that we have described here touch all corners of society. We now live in a world in which environmental deterioration, social inequality, poverty, and political upheaval are constants. And people from all walks of life will need to work together to solve these problems. We have already seen successful teams follow the X-team principles in the social sector, in government, and in groups that mesh government, private sector, and nongovernmental members. We expect to see these principles benefit teams of every stripe that are charged with solving the challenging and complex problems we now face.

X-teams will increasingly become the modus operandi wherever innovation, adaptation, and flexibility are prerequisites. The X-team is the perfect vehicle for reaching out to far-flung islands of expertise and information and for creating new synergies across units and organizations.

It is a vehicle to connect and align multiple people inside and outside the organization.

Yes, choosing to create X-teams in an organization will challenge everyone—from the individual team members involved to top management to the organization as a whole. Yet consider the many rewards, as we've illustrated them throughout this book—in organizations as diverse as Motorola and Microsoft, Southwest Airlines and Oxfam. "Never doubt that a small group of thoughtful, committed citizens can change the world," the famous American anthropologist Margaret Mead once said. "Indeed, it is the only thing that ever has."[16] That is the essential message and truth behind X-teams.

## Introduction

1. Paul Davidson is not his real name.
2. The term "distributed leadership" first appears in T. Malone, *The Future of Work* (Boston: Harvard Business School Press, 2004).
3. S. Levy, "Microsoft gets a clue from its Kiddie Corps," *Newsweek*, February 24, 2003.
4. T. Malone, *The Future of Work* (Boston: Harvard Business School Press, 2004).
5. D. G. Ancona and D. F. Caldwell, "Bridging the Boundary: External Activity and Performance in Organizational Teams," *Administrative Science Quarterly* 37 (1992): 634–665.
6. The three stages model was first introduced in D. G. Ancona and D. F. Caldwell, "Making Teamwork Work: Boundary Management in Product Development Teams," in *Managing Strategic Innovation and Change, A Collection of Readings*, ed. Michael L. Tushman and Philip Anderson (New York: Oxford University Press, 1997), 433–442.

## Chapter 1

1. J. R. Katzenbach and D. K. Smith, *The Wisdom of Teams* (Boston: Harvard Business School Press, 1993).
2. Compare Elaine Biech, ed., *The Pfeiffer Book of Successful Team-Building Tools* (San Francisco: John Wiley, 2001).
3. E. H. Schein, *Process Consultation Revisited: Building the Helping Relationship* (Reading, MA: Addison-Wesley, 1999); L. A. Hill, "Building Effective One-on-One Work Relationships," Harvard Business School Note 497-028.
4. M. D. Hanlon, D. A. Nadler, and D. L. Gladstein, *Attempting Work Reform: The Case of "Parkside" Hospital* (New York: Wiley & Sons, 1985).
5. Ibid.
6. D. L. Gladstein, "Groups in Context: A Model of Task Group Effectiveness," *Administrative Science Quarterly* 29 (1984): 499–517.
7. D. G. Ancona and D. F. Caldwell, "Bridging the Boundary: External Activity and Performance in Organizational Teams," *Administrative Science Quarterly* 37 (1992): 634–665.

8. D. G. Ancona, "Outward Bound: Strategies for Team Survival in an Organization," *Academy of Management Journal* 33 (1990): 334–365; D. G. Ancona and H. Bresman, "Begging, Borrowing and Building on Ideas from the Outside to Create Pulsed Innovation Inside Teams," in *Creativity and Innovation in Organizational Teams*, ed. L. Thompson and H. S. Choi (Mahwah, NJ: Lawrence Erlbaum, 2005), 183–198; H. Bresman, "Lessons Learned and Lessons Lost: A Multi-Method Field Study of Vicarious Team Learning Behavior and Performance," Academy of Management Best Paper Proceedings, Atlanta, August 2006.

9. J. S. Bunderson and K. M. Sutcliffe, "Why Some Teams Emphasize Learning More Than Others: Evidence from Business Unit Management Teams," in *Research on Managing Groups and Teams*, ed. E. A. Mannix and H. Sondak, 4th ed. (New York: Elsevier Science, 2002), 49–84; J. N. Cummings, "Work Groups, Structural Diversity, and Knowledge Sharing in a Global Organization," *Management Science* 50 (2004): 352–364; S. S. Wong, "Distal and Local Group Learning: Performance Trade-Offs and Tensions," *Organization Science* 15 (2004): 645–656; M. Zellmer-Bruhn, "Interruptive Events and Team Knowledge Acquisition," *Management Science* 49 (2003): 514–528.

10. Quotations from Sam and Ned come from interviews conducted by one of the authors in 1988.

11. C. P. Alderfer, "Boundary Relations and Organizational Diagnosis," in *Humanizing Organizational Behavior*, ed. M. Meltzer and F. Wickert (Springfield, IL: Charles C. Thomas), 142–175.

## Chapter 2

1. W. Whyte, *The Organization Man* (New York: Doubleday, 1956).

2. T. Malone, *The Future of Work* (Boston: Harvard Business School Press, 2004).

3. Ibid.

4. D. Carpenter, Associated Press, "Razr, Design Push Remake Motorola's Stodgy Image," April 9, 2005.

5. A disclaimer: the description of Razr is solely based on secondary sources. Since we started to write this book, and in the wake of Razr's success, numerous articles on this team have been published, not all of which are consistent. Our account draws particularly heavy on S. D. Anthony, "Making the Most of a Slim Chance," *Strategy and Innovation*, July–August 2005.

6. Information and quotations from Jeffrey Immelt are from E. Schonfeld, "GE Sees the Light," *Business 2.0*, July 2004.

7. G. Hedlund, "The modern MNC: A heterarchy?" *Human Resource Management* 25 (1986): 9-36; J. Birkinshaw, "Entrepreneurship in Multinational Corporations: The Characteristics of Subsidiary Initiatives, *Strategic Management Journal* 18 (1997): 207-229.

8. The company's real name has been disguised.

9. A. Pollack, "Despite Billions for Discoveries, Pipeline of Drugs Is Far from Full," *New York Times*, April 19, 2002.

10. This metaphor was first used in P. Hagström and G. Hedlund, "A Three-Dimensional Model of Changing Internal Structure in the Firm," in *The Dynamic*

*Firm*, ed. A. D. Chandler, P. Hagström, and Ö. Sölvell (Oxford, UK: Oxford University Press, 1998).

11. For more on the forces behind the changing knowledge structure and its effect on organizations, see G. Hedlund, "A model of knowledge management and the N-form corporation," *Strategic Management Journal* 15 (1994): 73–90.

12. D. Ancona, T. Malone, W. Orlikowski, P. Senge, "In Praise of the Incomplete Leader," *Harvard Business Review*, February 2007.

# Chapter 3

1. Big Bank team is not its real name.

2. K. Weick, *Sensemaking in Organizations* (Thousand Oaks, CA: SAGE Publications, 1995).

3. A. D. Grove, *Only the Paranoid Survive: How to Exploit the Crisis Points That Challenge Every Company* (New York: Doubleday, 1996). In addition to Andrew Grove, a number of researchers have written about revolutionary change and discontinuities. For example, see M. L. Tushman and E. Romanelli, "Organizational Evolution: A Metamorphosis Model of Convergence and Reorientation," in *Research in Organizational Behavior*, ed. L. L. Cummings and B. M. Staw (Greenwich, CT: JAI Press, 1985), 171–222.

4. For more on vicarious team learning, see H. Bresman, "Lessons Learned and Lessons Lost: A Multi-Method Field Study of Vicarious Team Learning Behavior and Performance," Academy of Management Best Paper Proceedings, Atlanta, August 2006.

5. S. D. Anthony, "Making the Most of a Slim Chance," *Strategy and Innovation*, July–August 2005.

6. D. G. Ancona and D. F. Caldwell, "Bridging the Boundary: External Activity and Performance in Organizational Teams," *Administrative Science Quarterly* 37 (1992): 634–665.

7. For more on transitions in teams, see C. J. G. Gersick, "Time and Transition in Work Teams," *Academy of Management Journal* 31 (1988): 9–41; J. R. Hackman and R. Wageman, "A Theory of Team Coaching," *Academy of Management Review* 30 (2005): 269–287.

8. D. G. Ancona and M. J. Waller, "The Dance of Entrainment: Temporally Navigating across Multiple Pacers," in *Research in the Sociology of Work*, ed. B. A. Rubin (Amsterdam: JAI, Elsevier Press, forthcoming).

9. D. G. Ancona and D. F. Caldwell, "Bridging the Boundary: External Activity and Performance in Organizational Teams," *Administrative Science Quarterly* 37 (1992): 634–665.

10. This and other quotations about the Razr team can be found in S. D. Anthony, "Making the Most of a Slim Chance," *Strategy and Innovation*, July–August 2005.

11. D. G. Ancona and D. F. Caldwell, "Bridging the Boundary: External Activity and Performance in Organizational Teams," *Administrative Science Quarterly* 37 (1992): 634–665.

12. B. A. Bechky, "In Working Order: Coordination Across Occupational Groups in Organizations," working paper, Graduate School of Management, USC Davis, 2006.

## Chapter 4

1. Both Gerhard Koepke and Powercorp are fictitious names.
2. A. C. Edmondson, "Psychological Safety and Learning Behavior in Work Teams," *Administrative Science Quarterly* 44 (1999): 350–383.
3. J. Pfeffer, "How Companies Get Smart," *Business 2.0*, February 2005.
4. J. H. Gittell, "Supervisory Span, Relational Coordination, and Flight Departure Performance: A Reassessment of Postbureaucracy Theory," *Organization Science* 12 (2001): 468–483.
5. Information and quotations about the hospital study came from Edmondson, "Psychological Safety and Learning Behavior in Work Teams," *Administrative Science Quarterly* 44 (1999): 350–383.
6. Information and quotations about Team EcoInternet came from C. Dahle, "Extreme Teams," *Fast Company*, November 1999.
7. For a review, see G. M. Wittenbaum and G. Stasser, "Management of Information in Small Groups," in *What's Social About Social Cognition? Research on Socially Shared Cognition in Small Groups*, ed. J. L. Nye and A. M. Brower (Thousand Oaks, CA: SAGE, 1996), 3–28.
8. This anecdote comes from E. Schonfeld, "GE Sees the Light," *Business 2.0*, July 2004.
9. M. A. West, "Reflexivity and Work Group Effectiveness: A Conceptual Integration," in *Handbook of Work Group Psychology*, ed. M. A. West (Chichester, UK: Wiley, 1996), 555–579.
10. J. R. Hackman and R. Wageman, "A Theory of Team Coaching," *Academy of Management Review* 30 (2005): 269–287.
11. E. H. Schein, *Process Consultation Revisited: Building the Helping Relationship* (Reading, MA: Addison-Wesley, 1999).
12. D. W. Wegner, "Transactive Memory: A Contemporary Analysis of the Group Mind," in *Theories of Group Behavior*, ed. B. Mullen and G. R. Goethals (New York: Springer-Verlag, 1987), 185–208.
13. This quotation and other information about Razr in this chapter comes from S. D. Anthony, "Making the Most of a Slim Chance," *Strategy and Innovation*, July–August 2005.
14. Information and quotations about Industrial Light & Magic came from C. Dahle, "Extreme Teams," *Fast Company*, November 1999.
15. J. R. Hackman and R. Wageman, "Total Quality Management: Empirical, Conceptual and Practical Issues," *Administrative Science Quarterly* 40 (1995): 309–342.
16. E. Matson, "Four Rules for Fast Teams," *Fast Company*, September 1996.
17. Example from M. A. Cusumano, "How Microsoft Makes Large Teams Work Like Small Teams," *MIT Sloan Management Review* 39, no. 1 (1997): 9-20.
18. H. Silove, "Discovering the Art of Innovation," *Business Day*, January 26, 2004.
19. Others have explored establishing rhythms for output: D. G. Ancona and C. L. Chong, "Cycles and Synchrony: The Temporal Role of Context in Team Behavior," in *Research on Managing Groups and Teams*, ed. R. Wageman (Stamford, CT: JAI Press, 1999), 33–48; K. M. Eisenhardt and S. L. Brown, "Time Pacing: Competing in Markets That Won't Stand Still," *Harvard Business Review*, March–April 1998, 59–69.

20. W. J. Holstein, "DaimlerChrysler's Net Designs," *Business 2.0*, April 2001.

21. "Brain Teasing," *Economist*, October 13, 2005.

22. F. Warner, "He Drills for Knowledge," *Fast Company*, September 2001.

## Chapter 5

1. The ProPoint team example has previously been described in D. G. Ancona and D. F. Caldwell, "Bridging the Boundary: External Activity and Performance in Organizational Teams," *Administrative Science Quarterly* 37 (1992): 634–665.

2. D. G. Ancona, "Outward Bound: Strategies for Team Survival in an Organization," *Academy of Management Journal* 33 (1990): 334–365; C. J. G. Gersick, "Time and Transition in Work Teams," *Academy of Management Journal* 31 (1988): 9–41; L. Thompson, *Making the Team* (Upper Saddle River, NJ: Prentice Hall, 2000).

3. D. G. Ancona, "Outward Bound: Strategies for Team Survival in an Organization," *Academy of Management Journal* 33 (1990): 334–365; D. G. Ancona and D. F. Caldwell, "Bridging the Boundary: External Activity and Performance in Organizational Teams," *Administrative Science Quarterly* 37 (1992): 634–665.

4. D. Ancona, T. Malone, W. Orlikowski, and P. Senge, "In Praise of the Incomplete Leader," *Harvard Business Review*, February 2007.

5. K. Weick, *Sensemaking in Organizations* (Thousand Oaks, CA: SAGE Publications, 1995).

6. Tom Roszko, interview by authors in New York, NY, 2004.

7. K. Weick, *Sensemaking in Organizations* (Thousand Oaks, CA: SAGE Publications, 1995).

8. See, for example, C. J. Nemeth and J. Kwan, "Minority Influence, Divergent Thinking and the Detection of Correct Solutions," *Journal of Applied Social Psychology* 17 (1987): 786–797.

## Chapter 6

1. H. R. Clinton, *It Takes a Village* (New York: Touchstone, 1996).

2. Quotations in this chapter from Tammy Savage are from an interview by the authors, Redmond, Washington, summer 2004.

3. C. Y. Chen, "Chasing the Net Generation," *Fortune,* September 4, 2000.

4. Quotations in this chapter from Kathleen Mulcahy are from an interview by the authors, Boston, Massachusetts, summer 2004.

5. M. Granovetter, "The Strength of Weak Ties," *American Journal of Sociology* 78 (1973): 1360–1380.

6. D. G. Ancona and D. F. Caldwell, "Composing Teams to Assure Successful Boundary Activity," in *Basic Principles of Organizational Behavior: A Handbook*, ed. E. A. Locke (Oxford, UK: Blackwell, 2000); D. G. Ancona, H. Bresman, and K. Kaeufer, "The Comparative Advantage of X-Teams," *MIT Sloan Management Review* 43, no. 3 (2002): 33–39.

7. From an interview by the authors, Redmond, Washington, summer 2004.

## Chapter 7

1. For a recent review of this stream of research, see R. E. Reagans, E. Zuckerman, and B. McEvily, "How to Make the Team: Social Networks vs. Demography as Criteria for Designing Effective Teams," *Administrative Science Quarterly* 49 (2004): 101–133.

2. K. Bettenhausen and J. K. Murnighan, "The Emergence of Norms in Competitive Decision-Making Groups," *Administrative Science Quarterly* 30 (1985): 350–372; C. J. G. Gersick, "Time and Transition in Work Teams," *Academy of Management Journal* 31 (1988): 9–41.

3. R. I. Sutton and A. Hargadon, "Brainstorming groups in context: Effectiveness in a product design firm," *Administrative Science Quarterly* 41 (1996): 685-718.

## Chapter 8

1. Quotations in this chapter from BP come from the BP Project Academy Recommendation Report, 2004.

2. This term first appeared in D. G. Ancona, G. Okhuysen, and L. Perlow, "Time Out: Taking Time to Integrate Temporal Research," *Academy of Management Review* 26 (2001): 512–529.

3. The information on Ford is from interviews by one of the authors with senior product development executives from the company who visited MIT in spring 2004.

## Chapter 9

1. As told by Jim Parker, the former CEO of Southwest Airlines, at a visit to the MIT Sloan School of Management in 2005.

2. Our description of Procter & Gamble in this chapter draws heavily on two secondary sources in particular: L. Huston and N. Sakkab, "Connect and Develop," *Harvard Business Review*, March 2006; E. Schonfeld, "P&G's Growth Wizard," *Business 2.0*, February 2005.

3. E. Schonfeld, "P&G's Growth Wizard," *Business 2.0*, February 2005.

4. L. Huston and N. Sakkab, "Connect and Develop," *Harvard Business Review*, March 2006.

5. D. Ancona, T. Malone, W. Orlikowski, and P. Senge, "In Praise of the Incomplete Leader," *Harvard Business Review*, February 2007, 2.

6. K. Weick, *Sensemaking in Organizations* (Thousand Oaks, CA: SAGE Publications, 1995).

7. L. Huston and N. Sakkab, "Connect and Develop," *Harvard Business Review*, March 2006.

8. E. H. Schein, *Organizational Culture and Leadership*, 3rd ed. (San Francisco: Jossey-Bass, 2004).

9. N. Repenning, "Understanding Fire Fighting in New Product Development," *Journal of Product Innovation Management* 18, no. 5 (2001): 285–300.

10. C. A. O'Reilly III and M. L. Tushman, "The Ambidextrous Organization," *Harvard Business Review*, April 2004, 74–81.

11. H. W. Chesbrough, "The Era of Open Innovation," *MIT Sloan Management Review* 44, no. 3 (2003): 35–41.

12. This term first appeared in D. G. Ancona, G. Okhuysen, and L. Perlow, "Time Out: Taking Time to Integrate Temporal Research," *Academy of Management Review* 26 (2001): 512–529.

13. L. Perlow, "The Time Famine: Towards a Sociology of Work Time," *Administrative Science Quarterly* 44 (1999): 57–81.

14. E. H. Schein, *Organizational Culture and Leadership*, 3rd ed. (San Francisco: Jossey-Bass, 2004).

15. T. Friedman, "It's a Flat World, After All," *New York Times*, April 3, 2005.

16. For this and countless other colorful quotes from Margaret Mead, see http://en .wikiquote.org/wiki/Margaret_Mead.

*Deborah Ancona* is the Seley Distinguished Professor of Management at the MIT Sloan School of Management, and Faculty Director of the MIT Leadership Center. She has consulted on leadership and innovation to premier companies such as AT&T, BP, CVRD, Merrill Lynch, and Newscorp.

Deborah's pioneering research into how successful teams operate has highlighted the critical importance of "managing outside the team's boundary as well as inside it." This research has led directly to the concept of X-Teams as a vehicle for driving innovation within large organizations.

Deborah's work has also focused on the concept of "distributed leadership" and the development of research-based tools, practices, and teaching/coaching models that enable organizations to foster creative leadership at every level. This work was highlighted in a recent article in the *Harvard Business Review*, "In Praise of the Incomplete Leader," February 2007.

Deborah's studies of team performance have also been published in the *Administrative Science Quarterly*, the *Academy of Management Journal*, *Organization Science*, and the *MIT Sloan Management Review*. Her previous book, *Managing for the Future: Organizational Behavior and Processes* (South-Western College Publishing, 1999, 2005), centers on the skills and processes needed in today's diverse and changing organization.

Deborah received her BA and MS in psychology from the University of Pennsylvania and her PhD in management from Columbia University.

*Henrik Bresman* is an Assistant Professor of Organizational Behavior at INSEAD, where he teaches MBA and executive courses in organizational leadership, technology innovation, and change management. His research at INSEAD focuses on high-performance teams, innovation, and leadership.

Professor Bresman received his PhD from the Massachusetts Institute of Technology, where he studied as a Fulbright scholar. He also holds a degree in economics from the Stockholm School of Economics. His PhD dissertation on strategically important innovation teams showed how high-performing teams were distinguished by their boundary-spanning activities and, in particular, by how they engaged in learning processes involving external actors. The dissertation was recognized by the Academy of Management with the William H. Newman Award, and his research has been published in several leading journals, such as the *MIT Sloan Management Review*.

Prior to joining INSEAD, Professor Bresman held a number of managerial, consulting, and entrepreneurial positions. Born and raised in Sweden, he currently resides in France.

HD66/.A518/2007
X-teams : how to build teams that lead, innovate,
and succeed.